THE MISSION OF JESUS THE MESSIAH

THE MISSION OF JESUS THE MESSIAH

E. KEITH HOWICK

WindRiver Publishing
St. George, Utah

Queries, comments or correspondence concerning this work should be directed to
the author and submitted to WindRiver Publishing at:

authors@windriverpublishing.com

Information regarding this work and other works published by WindRiver Publishing
Inc., and instructions for submitting manuscripts for review for publication, can be
found at:

www.windriverpublishing.com

The Mission of Jesus the Messiah
Copyright © 2003 by WindRiver Publishing, Inc.

Library of Congress Control Number: 2003102366
ISBN 1-886249-03-2 (previously published by Bookcraft, Inc., ISBN 0-88494-760-2)

First Printing, 1990
Second Printing, 2003

Printed on acid-free paper by Malloy, Inc., Ann Arbor MI, the United States of America

To Cindi and Christopher

Key to Abbreviations

Abbreviation	Name of Work
AF	James E. Talmage, *The Articles of Faith* (Salt Lake City, Deseret Book Company, 1955).
Bruce	Alexander Balmain Bruce, *The Training of the Twelve*, reprint ed. (Grand Rapids, Michigan: Kregel Publications, 1982).
DNTC	Bruce R. McConkie, *Doctrinal New Testament Commentary*, Vol. 1, *The Gospels* (Salt Lake City: Bookcraft, 1975).
Ed	Alfred Edersheim, *The Life and Times of Jesus the Messiah*, reprint ed. (Grand Rapids, Michigan: Wm. B. Eerdmans Publishing Company, 1981).
Ed BHOT	Alfred Edersheim, *Bible History — Old Testament*, reprint ed. (Grand Rapids, Michigan: Wm. B. Eerdmans Publishing Company, 1982).
Ed Temple	Alfred Edersheim, *The Temple: Its Ministry and Services As They Were at the Time of Jesus Christ*, reprint ed. (Grand Rapids, Michigan: Wm. B. Eerdmans Publishing Company, 1982).
Farrar	Frederic W. Farrar, *The Life of Christ*, 2 vols. (New York: E. P. Dutton and Company, 1874).
Geikie	Cunningham Geikie, *The Life and Words of Christ*, revised ed., 2 vols. (New York: D. Appleton and Company, 1891, 1894).

HC	Joseph Smith, Jr., *History of The Church of Jesus Christ of Latter-day Saints*, ed. B. H. Roberts, 7 vols. (Salt Lake City: The Church of Jesus Christ of Latter-day Saints, 1955).
JC	James E. Talmage, *Jesus the Christ* (Salt Lake City: Deseret Book Company, 1959).
JFS	Joseph Fielding Smith, *Doctrines of Salvation*, comp. Bruce R. McConkie, Vol. 1 (Salt Lake City: Bookcraft, 1959).
Josephus	Flavius Josephus, *Josephus: Complete Works*, trans. William Whiston (Grand Rapids, Michigan: Kregel Publications, 1971).
MD	Bruce R. McConkie, *Mormon Doctrine* (Salt Lake City: Bookcraft, 1966).
Mill M	Bruce R. McConkie, *The Millennial Messiah* (Salt Lake City: Deseret Book Company, 1978).
Miracles	E. Keith Howick, *The Miracles of Jesus the Messiah* (Salt Lake City: Bookcraft, 1985).
MM	Bruce R. McConkie, *The Mortal Messiah*, 4 vols. (Salt Lake City: Deseret Book Company, 1979–81).
Parables	E. Keith Howick, *The Parables of Jesus the Messiah* (Salt Lake City: Bookcraft, 1986).
Sermons	E. Keith Howick, *The Sermons of Jesus the Messiah* (Salt Lake City: Bookcraft, 1987).
SJSL	Alfred Edersheim, *Sketches of Jewish Social Life in the Days of Christ*, reprint ed.

(Grand Rapids, Michigan: Wm. B. Eerd-mans Publishing Company, 1982).

Smith   William Smith, *A Dictionary of the Bible*, rev. and ed. by F. N. and M. A. Peloubet (New York: Thomas Nelson Publishing, 1984).

TPJS   Joseph Smith, Jr., *Teachings of the Prophet Joseph Smith*, sel. Joseph Fielding Smith (Salt Lake City: Deseret Book Company, 1958).

Trench   Richard Chenevix Trench, *Notes on the Miracles of Our Lord* (Westwood, New Jersey: Fleming H. Revell Company, n.d.).

WMC   Walter M. Chandler, *The Trial of Jesus from a Lawyer's Standpoint*, Vol. 1, The Hebrew Trail (New York City: The Federal Book Co., 1925).

Contents

Introduction

Jesus taught and established his claim to the Messiahship with miracles, parables, and sermons,[1] but his ultimate purpose for coming to this earth was his mission.

The mission of Jesus the Messiah is revealed in the New Testament record of a series of events which took place during his earthly life. These events, beginning with his birth and ending with his resurrection and ascension, are recorded by the Gospel writers to substantiate their testimony of his divinity. In addition, several other events occurred during his mission that the Gospel writers alluded to but did not describe in detail. These events include his work in the premortal existence "Before the World Was," and in his work in "Old Testament times" when he was known as Jehovah (chapter 1); events that occurred between his death and resurrection, "In the World of Spirits" (chapter 8); his visit to the Western Hemisphere's "Other Sheep," "The Restoration" of the gospel in the latter days, and "The Second Coming of Jesus the Messiah" in the Millennium (chapter 10). These events, along with those described by Matthew, Mark, Luke, and John, comprise his mission.

Discussing the mission of Jesus is not like discussing the miracles, the parables, or the sermons. Those subjects had a predetermined boundary, each with a beginning and an end. The events of the Lord's mission were also described by the Gospel writers with a beginning and an end, but they have limitless consequences. These events range from the very beginning of the plan of salvation (as presented by the Father in the premortal spirit world) to the culmination of all things—the final judgment and beyond.

The main text for my discussion of the Lord's mission is the New Testament. No other known record describes the earthly life of the Lord in detail. However, it was not the intent of the Gospel writers to record a biography of Jesus. They did not describe his life, but his ministry. They did not testify of his life, but of his divinity. As they did with the miracles, the parables, and the sermons, the authors of the New Testament testified of Christ's mission and bore witness that he was the Messiah, the Son of God.[2]

Each author recorded the events of Christ's mission in a different manner, a fact that testifies of the Gospels' independent authorship. However, Matthew, Mark, and Luke (commonly referred to as the synoptic Gospels, or the Synoptics) do deal with the life of Christ in a similar manner, that is, they record many of the events of the mission in common. Although John records some events in common with the Synoptics, he also records many others not mentioned by them. In addition to the Gospels, the Book of Mormon describes and testifies of many of these events and serves as another testament for Jesus Christ. In fact, in three specific instances (the Crucifixion, the Resurrection, and the Lord's visit to his "other sheep"), the Book of Mormon leaves an extraordinary witness and testimony of the Savior's mission.

The classification and organization of the events in the Lord's mission as described in this book are my own. I have discussed these events in chronological order, beginning with the pre-earth mission of Jesus, culminating at his death and resurrection, and concluding with the Restoration and the Millennial advent. The scriptural story of each event is included in the text, but it is the doctrinal teaching that is emphasized and discussed. Also included are related teachings and examples that the Lord used throughout his ministry, testimony of Old Testament prophets and writings, and the scriptural and historical insight that other knowledgeable writers have given on the circumstances of his mission.

The body of the book is divided into four parts and eleven chapters. Chapters 1–10 deal with the events of the mission of Jesus; chapter 11 deals with the general message and importance of that mission.

All biblical references are from the standard King James Version unless otherwise stated. Each discussion begins with the relevant scripture text quoted in its entirety. (Only the principal text is used; duplicate descriptions are given as cross-references only.) Please note that when any part of a quoted scripture is discussed in the chapter dealing with that scripture, it is not referenced in that discussion (the whole relevant text having already been given). Cross-references are treated similarly. Cross-references to the Joseph Smith Translation of the Bible, which was formerly referred to as the "Inspired Version," are shown here as JST.

In discussing the trials of Jesus, I have combined the four Gospels (eliminating duplications) to provide a "scriptural story" of those events (chapter 7). This makes possible a very complete description of the trials.

The *mission* of Jesus is an integral part of the plan of salvation —the plan that was presented by the Father in the pre-earth existence and that is our purpose for being. Each event in Christ's mission testifies of him as the Messiah, not only for those who lived at Christ's time but also for all those who would follow.

The miracles of Jesus caused astonishment and wonder; his parables animated his teachings and simplified their understanding; his sermons gave gospel instruction and expounded doctrines of the kingdom of God. They were all used to teach and to testify and to proclaim Christ as the Son of God, but it was the events of his mission that bore the greatest witness of Jesus the Messiah.

Part One

"Here Am I,
Send Me"

In the Beginning   1

Before the World Was — The Plan

John 1:1-5

1. In the beginning was the Word, and the Word was with God, and the Word was God.

2. The same was in the beginning with God.

3. All things were made by him; and without him was not any thing made that was made.

4. In him was life; and the life was the light of men.

5. And the light shineth in darkness; and the darkness comprehended it not.

John begins his gospel with the declaration, "In the beginning was the Word, and the Word was with God, and the Word was God." The beginning, spoken of by John, was the time and place in which all God's spirit children dwelt prior to this earth. This time is referred to as the preexistence, or our premortal life, and is a place where as spirits "we were in all respects as we are now save only that we were not housed in mortal bodies."[1] The Word spoken of was none other than Jesus Christ,[2] who was the firstborn spirit son of the living God, our Father in Heaven.

Paul declared with fervor to the Hebrews that we "had fathers of our flesh which corrected us, and we gave them reverence: shall we not much rather be in subjection unto the Father of spirits, and live?" (Hebrews 12:9.) Therefore, God the Eternal Father, "whom we designate by the exalted name-title 'Elohim,' is the literal parent of our Lord and Savior Jesus Christ, and of [all] the spirits of the human race."[3] In this premortal state the entire human race existed as spirit beings in the presence of our Father in Heaven who, at some previous time, had passed through a mortal life of His own, including death and resurrection.[4]

Our birth order in premortality is unknown to us and unimportant, but Christ is designated as the firstborn of the Father. Undoubtedly all God's spirit children came into being as conscious identities in their own appointed order[5] and, during the period of their spirit existence, developed an infinite variety and degree of talents.[6]

Our object as spirits was to become like the Father,[7] and for this purpose He ordained and established certain laws for our advancement and progress.[8] We, through our obedience, move along the path designated by our Father in Heaven toward his ultimate goal, for he has declared that his work and glory is "to bring to pass the immortality and eternal life of man" (Moses 1:39).

In the spirit existence, as in this mortal life, some were more intelligent than others and had varying degrees of ability and power.[9] Regardless of ability or intelligence, however, each spirit possessed his or her own agency — a power given to each individual by the Father.[10] The eternal law of free agency was the birthright of every individual spirit child of our Father in Heaven. Agency gave them the ability to act for themselves.[11]

Of our existence in this premortal state we know very little, and although certain specifics are revealed, even these are limited. Where such revelation is given it would appear that its main purpose is to shed light upon the premortal Godship of Jesus Christ.[12]

John the Revelator beheld in open vision limited scenes from this premortal life. From his description we know that not all of our premortal existence was happiness and peace, for he saw and described great contention, even a "war" in heaven (Revelation 12:7-9).

Apparently this heavenly conflict followed a great council held by the spirits and the Father prior to the creation of this earth. In this council our Father in Heaven presented his plan for the continued progression of his spirit children. For the most part, the plan was received with joy and jubilation (Job 38:4-7); however, there stood one in the council who was described as a son of the morning (Isaiah 14:12-15) and who, desiring self-aggrandizement,[13] wanted the glory of the Eternal Father for himself (Moses 4:1-4; Abraham 3:27-28). He not only objected to the Father's plan but also presented a modification that would result in his exaltation (while destroying the agency of man). At this time Jesus Christ, who had glory with our Father in Heaven before the world was (John 17:5), stepped forward and offered himself in conformity with the Father's plan, declaring "Father, thy will be done, and the glory be thine forever" (Moses 4:2). Satan's plan was rejected and Jesus was chosen and ordained "to sacrifice Himself, through labor, humiliation and suffering even unto death."[14] His sacrifice made it possible for man to be redeemed from the effects of sin and to receive exaltation through righteous achievement and the grace of God.

In the verses quoted the beginning of the written history of Jesus the Christ commenced.[15] Because Satan rebelled and would not accept the Father's plan; he was cast out. His banishment and fall was graphically recorded by the Old Testament prophet Isaiah, who witnessed this event in a vision from the Lord (Isaiah 14:12-15).[16] Of this event Moses recorded the Lord's words, "He became Satan, yea, even the devil, the father of all lies, to deceive and to blind men, and to lead them captive at his will, even as many as would not hearken unto my voice" (Moses 4:4).

Jesus assisted in casting Satan out (Moses 4:3), and under the direction of the Father and in accordance with the plan accepted by the council, he created this earth and all things thereon. "The Father operated in the work of creation through the Son, who thus became the executive through whom the will, commandment, or word of the Father was put into effect . . . The part taken by Jesus Christ in the creation, a part so prominent as to justify our calling Him the Creator, is set forth in many scriptures."[17]

Speaking of Jesus, Paul declared with boldness and clarity, "For by him were all things created, that are in heaven, and that are in earth, visible and invisible, whether they be thrones, or dominions, or principalities, or powers: all things were created by him, and for him: and he is before all things, and by him all things consist" (Colossians 1:16–17).

Although man's premortal existence and the important role Jesus Christ played in it were but dimly perceived by the multitudes who lived during Old Testament times,[18] the holy prophets of that time undoubtedly knew the truth of the Son's premortal glory and mission (Isaiah 6:8; Psalm 25:14; Amos 3:7). The evidence presented in the Holy Scriptures (which includes the Savior's prayer in Gethsemane to his Father: "Glorify thou me with thine own self with the glory which I had with thee before the world was" [John 17:5]), confirms that the man known as Jesus of Nazareth existed with the Father prior to his birth in the flesh and that while in that premortal state he was called and ordained by the Father (and accepted by us all) as the Savior and Redeemer of the world.

Old Testament Times — Jehovah

The eighth article of faith begins, "We believe the Bible to be the word of God as far as it is translated correctly." Although some have used that expression to suggest limiting the use of the Bible, there is no question that "The Church of Jesus Christ of Latter-day Saints accepts the Holy Bible as the foremost of her standard works, first among the books which have been proclaimed as her written guides in faith and doctrine."[19]

Scholars agree that the Bible is a collection of books written by many different authors and that, in many instances, the writing of those books was separated widely in time. Further, there is no question that the Jews at the time of the Lord's earthly mission were in possession of most, if not all, of the Old Testament scriptures and considered them to be authoritative. In addition, because Jesus and the Apostles quoted from these records frequently and designated them as scripture (John 5:39), they presumably were authentic in the form then current.

The first five books of the Bible were known among the Jews as the Torah and were designated as the written Law. They are also referred to as the Pentateuch, and their authorship is (and always has been) ascribed to Moses (Ezra 6:18; 7:6; Nehemiah 8:1; John

7:19). The Jews also had the writings of the other prophets, the poetic books, and other historical books.

When Moses ended his prophetic ministry on the earth, he commanded the priests and the Levites to preserve the scrolls containing the Law (which had been given to them by the Lord) in the ark of the covenant (Deuteronomy 31:9). The ancient Israelites managed to maintain this record in one form or another throughout the early history of their independent empires and captivity. It appears, however, that the written books of the Law had been lost or discarded prior to the reign of Josiah (about 640 B.C.). Hilkiah (a priest in the temple during Josiah's reign) found a "book of the law" (2 Chronicles 34:14) and had it read before the king. In the sixth century B.C. Cyrus, king of Persia, allowed the Jews in his kingdom to return to Jerusalem and rebuild the temple according to the law of God (Ezra 1:1-6; 7:1-7). Ezra returned to Jerusalem after the completion of the temple and has been given the credit for compiling the books of the Old Testament in existence at his time.[20]

From Ezra until Christ the Law remained essentially intact and was only added to by prophets who lived during that time. In addition, many other books (considered less authoritative) were available to the Jews at the time of Jesus.[21] It is from the teachings found in all of these works—the Law, the Prophets, the poetic books, and the historical works —that the chosen people acquired their anticipation of the coming forth of the Messiah. They may have disagreed among themselves as to the time and manner of his appearance, but there is no question that the certainty of the Messiah's coming was well established in the hopes and beliefs of the Jews of Christ's day.[22] Indeed, it might be said that the Old Testament and the history of the chosen people in its entirety were "symbolic, and typical of the future—the Old Testament the glass, through which the universal blessings of [the Messianic] days were seen."[23]

Because of the fall of Adam death came into the world, and man was by himself incapable of overcoming it. The plan of salvation, voted upon and accepted by the Father's righteous children in the great council in heaven, decreed that a future Redeemer would overcome death and make it possible for man to return to the Father's presence. In their fallen state, Adam and Eve had been driven from the Garden of Eden and were unable to enjoy the Father's continuous personal association. Sometime after leaving the Garden of Eden, Adam was instructed to offer sacrifice to the Lord. On one of those sacrificial occasions an angel of the Lord came to him inquiring, "Why dost thou offer sacrifices unto the Lord?" Adam responded, "I know not, save the Lord commanded me." His answer indicated that he had not yet been fully instructed concerning the purpose of sacrifice, so the angel proceeded to clearly outline the purpose of the sacrificial commandment by declaring: "This thing is a similitude of the sacrifice of the Only Begotten of the Father, which is full of grace and truth. Wherefore, thou shalt do all that thou doest in the name of the Son, and thou shalt repent and call upon God in the name of the Son forever more." (Moses 5:6–9.)

Sacrifice, as a prototype of the death of the future Messiah, was thus practiced not only from the time of Moses (as commanded by the Law) but also from the beginning of human history.[24] The Bible does not specifically designate the origin of sacrifice as prefiguring the atoning death of Jesus Christ,[25] but significant examples of this are found in the biblical stories of Cain and Abel (Genesis 4:3–4), of Noah's sacrifice after the Flood (Genesis 8:20), of the story of Abraham and Isaac (Genesis 22:2, 13), and the story of Jacob, the father of the house of Israel (Genesis 31:54; 46:1).

The "significance of the divinely established requirement [sacrifice] was explained in its fullness to the patriarch of the race [Adam]."[26] Its origin is based on specific revelation (Moses 5:5–8). Further, the prophets of the Old Testament understood the doctrines surrounding the coming forth of the Messiah. Job rejoiced at Christ's anticipated coming (Job 19:25–27), and the Psalms are replete with anticipation of his advent.[27] His coming was further attested to by Enoch (the father of Methuselah) (Moses 6:21, 52) and by the covenant of Abraham (which promised that through father Abraham's seed all nations of the earth would be blessed) (Genesis 12:3; 18:18; 22:18; 26:4; 28:14). Furthermore, the blessing given to Judah by his father, Israel, presaged the birth line of the Savior (Genesis 49:10).

Isaiah foretold the Messiah's virgin birth (Isaiah 7:14) and sang his praise as if it had already occurred (Isaiah 9:6–7). He declared the Savior's lineage as a branch from Jesse (Isaiah 11:1, 10); glorified him as the foundation stone of Zion (Isaiah 28:16), the Shepherd of the house of Israel (Isaiah 40:9-11), and the Light of the world (Isaiah 42:6); prophesied of John as his forerunner (Isaiah 40:3); and praised the Lord Jehovah as the leader and commander of both Jew and Gentile (Isaiah 55:4). Finally, in one sublime chapter he envisioned the Messiah of Israel in his ministry and portrayed his atonement and death (see Isaiah 53).

Other prophets of the Old Testament also received revelation and enlightenment pertaining to the Messiah's advent. Jeremiah knew and through revelation was assured of his safe advent (Jeremiah 23:5-6; 33:14-16). Ezekiel prophesied of him (Ezekiel 34:23; 37:24-25), as did Hosea (Hosea 11:1) and Micah (Micah 5:2). Zechariah saw Christ's triumphant entry into Jerusalem (Zechariah 9:9), noted that his own people would "pierce" their Savior (Zechariah 12:10), observed the Jews suffering centuries of trials and tribulations as they waited for their Messiah, and then heard them question the Savior concerning his wounds (Zechariah 13:6).

Moses, the great Lawgiver of Israel, prophesied of Christ and of the condemnation he would receive from those who would not accept him (Deuteronomy 18:15-19). From the great exodus forward, every paschal lamb slain at every Passover looked forward to Jesus as the Lamb of God.[28] Paul affirmed this conclusion to the Corinthians when he said, "For even Christ our passover is sacrificed for us" (1 Corinthians 5:7). All of these great visions and prophecies from the Old Testament were given by the Lord Jehovah to his ancient prophets.

When Moses spoke with the God of Abraham, Isaac, and Jacob on the holy mount, Moses asked him to declare his name so that he might properly identify God for the children of Israel. In response God said, "I AM THAT I AM," and he said, "Thus shalt thou say unto the children of Israel, I AM hath sent me unto you" (Exodus 3:14). During his earthly ministry Jesus used this name as his own, declaring to the unbelieving Jews, "Before Abraham was, I am" (John 8:58),[29] thus attesting to his divinity and revealing his identity to them. He was the same God that had communicated with Adam after the Garden of Eden, and with all of the prophets: Abraham, Isaac, Jacob, Moses, Isaiah, Jeremiah, Zechariah, and others — a fact that Paul also attested to when (speaking of those who lived during the time of Moses) he declared to the Corinthians that they "drank of that spiritual Rock that followed them: and that Rock was Christ" (1 Corinthians 10:4).

The Jewish leadership of Christ's day understood his claim. They knew that he was claiming to be the great Jehovah, God of the Old Testament, and in their anger and disgust they took "up stones to cast at him" (John 8:59).

It is the unqualified conviction of The Church of Jesus Christ of Latter-day Saints that Jehovah, God of the Old Testament, is and was Jesus Christ. "He was chosen and ordained to be the Savior of the unborn race of mortals, and Redeemer of a world then in its formative stages of development." He was "the God at whose instance the prophets of the ages have spoken, the God of all nations, and He who shall yet reign on earth as King of kings and Lord of lords," even Jesus the Messiah.[30]

"And the Word Was Made Flesh" 2

Galilee

In the days of King David, Galilee consisted of a circle of twenty cities in the circuit Kedesh-Naphtali. Hiram, the king of Tyre, had made an alliance of peace with David and had supplied him with artisans and timber for the palace and the temple of Jerusalem. Because of his services, Solomon, David's son, gave Hiram these twenty cities, but Hiram did not like the cities and called them "Cabul" (1 Kings 9:11-13), which meant "disgusting."[1] Because of this designation, perhaps, and due to the fact that the area readily associated itself geographically with a mixed population and with heathens, the people of Galilee were destined to be despised by their fellow Israelites.

The Galileans were looked upon with contempt (particularly by the Judeans) not only for their association with heathens but also for their less educated dialect and their lack of culture.[2] "The people of Galilee were especially blamed for neglecting the study of their language, charged with errors of grammar, and especially with absurd malpronunciation, sometimes leading to ridiculous mistakes."[3]

Three caravan trade routes passed through Palestine at the time of Christ, one of them through Nazareth, where he made his home. While Galilee was not the home of Rabbinism, its inhabitants were "of generous spirits, of warm, impulsive hearts, of intense nationalism, of simple manners, and of earnest piety."[4]

Anciently, Galilee contained the possessions of the tribes of Issachar, Zebulun, Naphtali, and Asher, but at the time of Christ it stretched beyond those boundaries and bordered Tyre and Syria to the north and Samaria to the south. Mount Carmel formed the western boundary, and the Jordan River and the Lake of Gennesaret the eastern.[5] It was a rich, fertile area and well cultivated.[6] Although this was perhaps exaggerated, it was reputed to be thickly populated, with as many as 240 towns and villages with not less than fifteen thousand inhabitants in each of them.[7]

Galilee was a gathering place or "priest-centre" for temple service[8] — a place of rich plains, luxuriant vegetation, fountains and rivers, and richly wooded hills.[9] Although the inhabitants were generally looked down upon and were not participants of the Rabbinic schools of Judea, they remained a thoroughly Jewish people.

Nestled in the mountains of lower Galilee and surrounded by fifteen hilltops that almost formed an amphitheater was the hamlet of Nazareth.[10] This community marked the northern boundary of ancient Zebulun, and just beyond it stretched the seemingly unbounded expanse of the Plain of Esdraelon, site of numerous battles of ancient Israel. It was a provincial village in a despised province of a conquered land, and in this obscure setting the long-awaited Messiah of the world made his home from the time of his return from Egypt until he entered his public ministry.

What Messiah Did the Jews Expect?

The Talmud states, "All the prophets prophesied only of the days of the Messiah," and "The world was created only for the Messiah."[11] Generally speaking, the whole of the Old Testament had become the perspective from which the Messianic expectation was envisioned.

It does not appear from the Gospel narratives that the leaders of the Jews took particular exception to Christ's fulfillment of individual prophecies relating to his claim to the Messiahship, but their general perception of the Messiah completely differed from what Jesus actually represented,[12] and therein lay the seeds for their rejection of him. Their anticipated Messiah was to perform "all the miracles and deliverances of Israel's past . . . only in a much wider manner," and thus the Old Testament was "the glass, through which the universal blessings of the latter days [the days of the Messiah] were seen."[13]

Israel was intensely interested in the restoration of its former glory, and the Messiah was the "grand instrument" they supposed would bring them to attain that goal. He was to be Israel's "exultation, rather than . . . the salvation of the world."[14] This purely political Messianic expectation was scarcely referred to by Jesus, and he deliberately separated himself from the popular Messianic beliefs and ideas of his time.[15]

It was to a people drunk with the vision of outward felicity and political greatness that Jesus came, and while some—such as Zacharias, Elisabeth, Mary, Anna, Simeon, and John the Baptist—heeded the coming of the Messiah's kingdom in its spiritual purity, the general belief was that he would come to restore the "splendour of the Jewish throne."[16] He would be a great prince who would found a great kingdom, a human hero who would lead Israel to victory and subdue all nations. Some even taught that "He would not know that He was the Messiah till Elias came . . . and anointed Him."[17]

The universal kingdom of the anticipated Messiah would be an earthly paradise, where "all the trees [would] bear continually. A single grape [would] load a waggon or a ship, and when it [was] brought to the house they [would] draw wine from it as from a cask. . . . The country round [would] be full of pearls and precious stones, so that Jews from all parts may come and take of them as they like."[18]

The Jews attached great mystery to the Messiah's birth and superhuman character traits to his mission.[19] Is it any wonder that the Rabbinic tradition found no place for Jesus as the Messiah? Jesus so completely separated himself from all of these ideas that there "was in such a Messiah [as Jesus] absolutely nothing—past, present, or possible; intellectually, religiously, or even nationally—to attract, but all to repel."[20] For the Messiah to be born to a virgin of Galilee who was betrothed to a humble carpenter would have been a caricature of the Jewish Messianic expectation, both unimaginable and unacceptable to the majority of the Jews of his day.

The details of Christ's birth as described in Matthew and Luke were contrary to the traditional and historical Jewish Messianic expectations, nor would their belief and interpretation of the Old Testament have corresponded to his simple advent.[21] Isaiah, the great prophet of old, had foreseen Israel's decay for century after century, so marked with turmoil and change that he could only describe the humble citizen of Nazareth, the heir to the throne of Israel, as a "root out of a dry ground" (Isaiah 53:2).

Joseph and Mary

Luke 1:26–35

26. And in the sixth month the angel Gabriel was sent from God unto a city of Galilee, named Nazareth,

27. To a virgin espoused to a man whose name was Joseph, of the house of David; and the virgin's name was Mary.

28. And the angel came in unto her, and said, Hail, thou that art highly favoured, the Lord is with thee: blessed art thou among women.

29. And when she saw him, she was troubled at his saying, and cast in her mind what manner of salutation this should be.

30. And the angel said unto her, Fear not, Mary: for thou hast found favour with God.

31. And, behold, thou shalt conceive in thy womb, and bring forth a son, and shalt call his name JESUS.

32. He shall be great, and shall be called the Son of the Highest: and the Lord God shall give unto him the throne of his father David:

33. And he shall reign over the house of Jacob for ever; and of his kingdom there shall be no end.

34. Then said Mary unto the angel, How shall this be, seeing I know not a man?

35. And the angel answered and said unto her, The Holy Ghost shall come upon thee, and the power of the Highest shall overshadow thee: therefore also that holy thing which shall be born of thee shall be called the Son of God.

Cross-references

Luke 1:36–80, 2:1–20   Matthew 1:18–25
Helaman 14:2   3 Nephi 1:9, 12–21

Three months had passed since the angel Gabriel had visited Zacharias in the temple and told him of the forthcoming birth of John, the forerunner of the Messiah (see chapter 3). While he and Elisabeth rejoiced at their home in the south, a hundred miles to the north in the village of Nazareth lived a just man (and a strict observer of the Law) named Joseph.[22]

Joseph was betrothed to a young Jewish maiden (perhaps only fifteen years of age)[23] named Mary. He was a carpenter by trade, and both he and Mary were poor,[24] even though they were descendants of the royal house of David.[25]

Christ has two genealogies recorded in the New Testament, one in Matthew and one in Luke. There are some discrepancies between the two. Whether the genealogies are considered those of Joseph and Mary[26] or whether they are both considered that of Joseph (which is the most accepted view),[27] it is still evident that both of their lines descended from the royal house. It is generally thought that Matthew's account is that of Joseph's royal lineage and that Luke's genealogy is his pedigree. Further, it is generally accepted that Joseph and Mary were cousins, one a descendant of Jacob and the other of Heli (brothers in the royal lineage).[28]

Jesus readily accepted the title "Son of David," denoting his royal lineage (Matthew 9:27; 15:22; 21:9; 20:30–31; Luke 18:38–39), a fact which Paul later confirmed several times (Romans 1:3; 2 Timothy 2:8; Acts 2:29–30; 13:22–23; compare Psalm 132:11; Luke 1:32). Further, of all the accusations laid against Jesus by his enemies, no mention or insinuation is given that he was not of the royal line.[29] The genealogies of the Jews were assiduously cared for,[30] and the Lord's enemies would have quickly made such an accusation if they could.

From the limited information we have about Joseph, it is evident that he was the rightful heir to the throne of Israel; because he and Mary were cousins, both descending from King David, Jesus was by birth the King of the Jews.

In those days, a betrothal was considered as binding as marriage. Once the betrothal was sealed with the customary prayer (and perhaps the statutory cup of wine tasted first by Joseph and then by Mary), the relationship was considered sacred, "as if they had already been wedded."[31] "The betrothal was formally made, with rejoicing, in the house of the bride, under a tent or slight canopy raised for the purpose. It was called 'making sacred,' as the bride, thenceforth, was sacred to her husband, in the strictest sense."[32] To make the betrothal legal, Joseph would have given his "betrothed a piece of money, or the worth of it, before witnesses."[33] The betrothal could be sealed either by solemn word of mouth or in a formal writing.[34] "Though betrothal was virtually marriage, and could only be broken off by a formal 'bill of divorcement,' the betrothed did not at once go to her husband's house . . . an interval elapsed before the final ceremony; [which] might be so many weeks, or months, or even a whole year."[35] There were two ways to annul a betrothal, both of which were akin to divorce. The first was by public trial and judgment, and the second was by a private agreement which was written and signed in the presence of witnesses.[36]

This was the condition of the relationship between Joseph and Mary, the unwed wife and virgin mother to be, when the angel Gabriel appeared. The time of day of the angelic visit is not given in the scriptures; however, as a devout Jewess knowing the Law, Mary would have been dutiful to her daily prayers, which occurred at the morning offering, at the noon hour, and at the evening sacrifice. Perhaps it was at one of these times that the angel Gabriel made his appearance.[37]

We can assume that Mary was prepared and personally worthy of his visit, because of the salutation that the angel gave her. The anticipated Messiah was not an abstract belief, it was considered a matter of certain fact;[38] and Mary certainly would have known that some Jewish maiden of the royal line was yet to become the mother of the Christ.[39] Her apparent bewilderment and surprise was not because Israel's great hope, the coming of the long-awaited Messiah, would now be fulfilled, but that it would be fulfilled through her. The angel greeted Mary with a well-known salutation[40] and revealed the great blessing that had been given her.

There was no hesitation in her response to the angel—her question merely voiced concern for her unwed status. "How shall this be, seeing I know not a man?" she asked. The angel answered by announcing the birth of the coming Savior—that birth would not be contrary to natural law, but it would also involve a higher law, for the Father of the Savior of the world would be Elohim,[41] thus giving Christ the combined powers of Godhood and of mortality.[42] The promise given by the Father to Adam and Eve (that through the seed of the woman Satan's head would be crushed) was about to be fulfilled (Genesis 3:15). The promised Savior, the Redeemer who could overcome Satan's power, was about to be born into mortality.

Mary was troubled. Her understanding of the significance of the event was as yet unclear. She "like all her nation [would have] thought of the Messiah as a Jewish king who should restore the long-lost glories of her race, and make Israel triumphant over all the heathen."[43] This belief would have been contradicted by the reality of his birth, for he was to be born as all mortals have been born—a mere babe that would grow from childhood to adulthood.[44] "It is apparent that the great truth as to the personality and mission of her divine Son had not yet unfolded itself in its fulness to her mind. The whole course of events, from the salutation of Gabriel to the reverent testimony of the shepherds concerning the announcing angel and the heavenly hosts, was largely a mystery to that stainless mother and wife."[45] The "almost universal belief was that He (the Messiah) was to be simply a man, who would receive miraculous endowments, on His formal consecration as Messiah."[46]

Mary's confusion apparently continued even as her divine Son was recognizing his mission, for she was obviously perplexed at his answer when she rebuked him at the age of twelve for staying behind at the temple following a visit to Jerusalem (Luke 2:48-50). When he became an adult she evidently misunderstood how his personal powers were to be used, for he mildly rebuked her when she implied that he should change water into wine (John 2:3-4). She and his immediate family apparently continued to misunderstand his mission (Mark 3:21, 31-32), and maintained the traditional view of the anticipated Messiah well into his ministry (John 7:1-8). Her realization of his position and power seemed to grow slowly through the years, just as it did for his disciples (Luke 24:13-25). This may have been due to the fact that the "preoccupation of the mind by fixed opinions, leads to a wrong reading of any evidence. We unconsciously distort facts, or invent them, to support our favourite theories, and see everything through their medium."[47] The evidence of the scriptures would indicate that Mary never seemed "to have fully understood her Son; at every new evidence of His uniqueness she marvelled and pondered anew."[48]

Mary had been told by the angel that her firstborn son was the Son of God, yet it would apparently be many years before she would even partially realize the importance of these words. Even the mother of the Savior of all mankind had to be led step by step to a final comprehension of his majesty.[49]

To Elisabeth and Bethlehem

Luke 1:36–56

36. And, behold, thy cousin Elisabeth, she hath also conceived a son in her old age: and this is the sixth month with her, who was called barren.

37. For with God nothing shall be impossible.

38. And Mary said, Behold the handmaid of the Lord; be it unto me according to thy word. And the angel departed from her.

39. And Mary arose in those days, and went into the hill country with haste, into a city of Juda;

40. And entered into the house of Zacharias, and saluted Elisabeth.

41. And it came to pass, that, when Elisabeth heard the salutation of Mary, the babe leaped in her womb; and Elisabeth was filled with the Holy Ghost:

42. And she spake out with a loud voice, and said, Blessed art thou among women, and blessed is the fruit of thy womb.

43. And whence is this to me, that the mother of my Lord should come to me?

44. For, lo, as soon as the voice of thy salutation sounded in mine ears, the babe leaped in my womb for joy.

45. And blessed is she that believed: for there shall be a performance of those things which were told her from the Lord.

46. And Mary said, My soul doth magnify the Lord,

47. And my spirit hath rejoiced in God my Saviour.

48. For he hath regarded the low estate of his handmaiden: for, behold, from henceforth all generations shall call me blessed.

49. For he that is mighty hath done to me great things; and holy is his name.

50. And his mercy is on them that fear him from generation to generation.

51. He hath shewed strength with his arm; he hath scattered the proud in the imagination of their hearts.

52. He hath put down the mighty from their seats, and exalted them of low degree.

53. He hath filled the hungry with good things; and the rich he hath sent empty away.

54. He hath holpen his servant Israel, in remembrance of his mercy;

55. As he spake to our fathers, to Abraham, and to his seed for ever.

56. And Mary abode with her about three months, and returned to her own house.

The angel Gabriel told Mary that her cousin Elisabeth[50] had also been blessed by the Lord and had conceived a son in her old age. With haste, Mary departed to visit Elisabeth to share in the joy extended to her formerly barren cousin and to tell her of the blessing she herself had received from God. The angel had informed Mary that Elisabeth was in her sixth month of pregnancy. Undoubtedly Elisabeth would have learned from Zacharias about the future calling of her yet unborn son and the near advent of the Messiah. However, it is equally apparent that she did not know (nor did Zacharias) when the Messiah would arrive or of whom he would be born.[51]

The Holy Ghost had moved upon Mary to prepare her for Gabriel's visit and for the conception of the Son of God, and He would now move upon Elisabeth and the yet unborn John to testify to them of that miraculous occurrence. Such activity by the Holy Ghost among the Jews was quite familiar in Israel at the time,[52] so Mary made haste to join her cousin Elisabeth.

In all probability Mary had told no one of the miraculous occurrence that had taken place,[53] and through her visit to Elisabeth both women would gain further understanding and testimony of the anticipated Messiah and his forerunner. The scriptures testify that upon Mary's arrival both Elisabeth and her yet unborn son were filled with the Holy Ghost. The child leapt within her womb as a sign and testimony of the coming Messiah. This also was an experience not strange to the Jewish expectancy.[54] Elisabeth's salutation to Mary was prophetic, for she recognized that Mary was the chosen mother of the Messiah and that she, Elisabeth, carried the child that would be his forerunner, a man whom the Christ would acclaim with the words, "Among those that are born of women there is not a greater prophet than John the Baptist" (Luke 7:28).

Mary's response was poetic, and "the rhythmical expression into which she falls was only what might have been expected from one imbued, as all Jewish minds were, with the style and imagery of the Old Testament."[55] After Elisabeth had praised Mary and her yet unborn son, Mary sang a song of praise to God in response to the salutation given her. This song was much like the songs women in Old Testament days had sung in times of joy: for example, Miriam at the passing of the Red Sea (Exodus 15:20–21), Deborah when she saved Israel from Sisera (Judges 5), and Hannah when she took the boy Samuel to Eli (1 Samuel 2:1–10). The poem was undoubtedly spontaneous and echoes the prophets and saints she had become familiar with through the imagery and language of the Old Testament. It testifies that she was well trained in the knowledge of the scriptures and gives a further indication of the spirit with which her sacred child would be trained.[56]

Mary stayed with Elisabeth until it was almost time for John to be born, then she returned to her home in Nazareth. When Joseph learned of her condition he pondered how best he could dissolve the betrothal; and rather than humiliate Mary with a public trial, which was one option, he "was minded to put her away privily" (Matthew 1:19).

Joseph's actions on this matter support the scriptural description of him as a just man. But before he could carry out his intent an angel appeared to him in a dream and testified of the divine parentage of Mary's child. To the Jews of that day "a good dream was . . . regarded as [a] mark of God's favour."[57] Consequently, Joseph was well disposed to receive the message that came in that manner. With the testimony of God's divine Son confirmed,

Joseph married Mary immediately so that no shame would come upon her.

Perhaps it was the intention of Joseph and Mary to remain in Nazareth after their marriage, but just as the circumstances surrounding the conception of the Messiah were beyond their control, so too were the circumstances that would make Bethlehem Christ's birthplace.[58]

Augustus, ruler of the Roman Empire, ordered an enrollment or census of all the Empire's provinces so that he might "know the number of soldiers he could levy in each, and the amount of taxes due to the treasury."[59] In all probability this census took years to complete, and in Judea it was undoubtedly left to Herod (as it would have been to all of the rulers of the individual provinces) to determine exactly how to accomplish the count.[60] Because of this, in the Roman province of Judea the citizens did not enroll their names at the town of their residence as the Romans did, but pursuant to Jewish custom they filed their registration in the ancestral home of their ancient or family tribes.[61] Joseph and Mary were of the lineage of David; therefore, they had to leave the mountains of Zebulun and travel some eighty miles along crisscrossed roads and paths that ran through many towns and cities and across the plain of Esdraelon before they reached the city of David — Bethlehem.

The journey must have taken at least three days, but no details of the trip are given in the scriptures. When they arrived in Bethlehem they had to search for shelter because the town was excessively crowded with those who had also come to register. The inns were full and the only available space was a cattle stable.[62] Such a place was not necessarily degrading, but in all probability was "half kitchen and half stable, which was simply one of the countless natural hollows or caves in the hill-side, against which the house had been built."[63] The hospitality of such a place was offered willingly as a religious merit, with the rabbinical promise of paradise as its reward.[64]

Thus the lovely Mary, lodging on hay and straw in a limestone grotto only a few miles from the splendor of Herod's palace — but far from her home and amidst strangers, in circumstances devoid of all earthly comfort and splendor — gave birth to the Lord Jesus Christ.

The hope of Israel had come! The promise of God, made unto the fathers, had been fulfilled! It was the event that all of Israel had earnestly sought for in their prayers and had painstakingly integrated into almost every event and activity in their lives.[65] The Sacred Child was born a Jew, his true paternity known to few, for he was regarded as the son of Joseph of Nazareth (Luke 4:22; Matthew 13:55; Mark 6:3). The narrative of his birth and the events surrounding it are so simple and lacking in detail that it is apparent the Gospel writers had no intention of providing a biography of Jesus Christ — their sole purpose was to witness to his divinity and generate belief in him.

The Testimony of Shepherds

Luke 2:8–20

8. And there were in the same country shepherds abiding in the field, keeping watch over their flock by night.

9. And, lo, the angel of the Lord came upon them, and the glory of the Lord shone round about them: and they were sore afraid.

10. And the angel said unto them, Fear not: for, behold, I bring you good tidings of great joy, which shall be to all people.

11. For unto you is born this day in the city of David a Saviour, which is Christ the Lord.

12. And this shall be a sign unto you; Ye shall find the babe wrapped in swaddling clothes, lying in a manger.

13. And suddenly there was with the angel a multitude of the heavenly host praising God, and saying,

14. Glory to God in the highest, and on earth peace, good will toward men.

15. And it came to pass, as the angels were gone away from them into heaven, the shepherds said one to another, Let us now go even unto Bethlehem, and see this thing which is come to pass, which the Lord hath made known unto us.

16. And they came with haste, and found Mary, and Joseph, and the babe lying in a manger.

17. And when they had seen it, they made known abroad the saying which was told them concerning this child.

18. And all they that heard it wondered at those things which were told them by the shepherds.

19. But Mary kept all these things, and pondered them in her heart.

20. And the shepherds returned, glorifying and praising God for all the things that they had heard and seen, as it was told unto them.

Immediately after reciting the birth of the Savior, Luke tells us of the divine witness received by the shepherds. Bethlehem was an agrarian area[66] so it was not uncommon to find shepherds on the hillsides tending their flocks. The biblical record gives no indication of the time of year in which Jesus was born. Some have pictured it during the chilly nights of winter;[67] others think it occurred in the early spring.[68] The flocks tended by the shepherds were probably not those of the common people but were more likely temple flocks. The temple shepherds would have been in the fields year round to provide sheep for the many temple ceremonies.[69]

Although his birth was practically unnoticed by mortals, the heavens openly rejoiced at the Savior's advent. On the slopes and heights of the hills surrounding Bethlehem the shepherds heard and saw the heavenly hosts celebrate that birth with hallelujah praises and song. The shepherds had neither asked for nor anticipated these signs —but they were blessed to receive them. And when they were told to go and see the newborn child for themselves they went in haste, their hearts in tune to receive this great blessing.[70] They confirmed the angels' testimony when they witnessed the babe lying in a manger; thereafter, they spread abroad all that they had both seen and heard (Luke 2:17). They undoubtedly told those in the inn and the residents of the countryside; possibly they told it also to those who worked in the temple area when they delivered their flocks for the sacrifices. Perhaps their message was instrumental in preparing the minds of Simeon and Anna for the witness that they too would bear.[71]

Another Testament of His Birth

Five years before the birth of Christ occurred on the Eastern Hemisphere another people an ocean away in a choice land were being testified to by Samuel the Lamanite about the coming birth of him who would provide their means of salvation. These people were also of the house of Israel, and through six hundred years of varying degrees of righteousness and wickedness they too had been looking forward to the Savior's advent. Now, five years before his birth, the Nephite people in the Americas were in a state of wickedness, and Samuel was prophesying and warning them about what was to come. He stood upon a wall and testified to them of their exceeding wickedness and the need for repentance. He gave them a sign of the coming Messiah. He told them that five years hence there would be a day, a night, and a day without darkness, and this miracle would occur at the time of Christ's birth (Helaman 14:2-5).

As the time approached, the wickedness of the people increased, and the prophet Nephi longed for the day when the sign would occur. The wicked also began to keep track of the time, but for a different reason — they threatened that if the sign did not take place by a certain day they would put to death all the members of the Church who believed (3 Nephi 1:5-9).

Nephi prayed fervently that the time might be made known and the Saints' lives spared. While he was praying, a voice from heaven declared that that night the sign would be given and the next day the Savior of the world would be born (3 Nephi 1:11-13). As the sun set and the day ended, darkness did not creep in — the land remained light as if it were noonday. This strange phenomenon continued all through the nocturnal hours until the sun again rose. As morning dawned, the Nephites and the Lamanites knew that the Redeemer of the world had come and that the testimony had been given to the Western Hemisphere as promised (3 Nephi 1:15-19).

In Compliance with the Law

Luke 2:21-24

21. And when eight days were accomplished for the circumcising of the child, his name was called JESUS,

which was so named of the angel before he was conceived in the womb.

22. And when the days of her purification according to the law of Moses were accomplished, they brought him to Jerusalem, to present him to the Lord;

23. (As it is written in the law of the Lord, Every male that openeth the womb shall be called holy to the Lord;)

24. And to offer a sacrifice according to that which is said in the law of the Lord, A pair of turtledoves, or two young pigeons.

Although we do not know how long Joseph and Mary remained in Bethlehem, as devout Jews they would have at least stayed long enough to comply with the requirements of the Levitical Law.

The first of these requirements (the ceremonial ritual of circumcision) was complied with eight days after the birth of the Savior. It was at this ceremony that he received the given name of Jesus. Jesus is the English translation or modification of the Hebrew name Joshua, which means "salvation is Jehovah."[72] The name represented his office and in Hebrew literally meant "the Messiah" (in Greek, "the Christ").[73] It was not necessary to attend the temple for a circumcision ceremony, because any rabbi could perform it; however, being so close to the temple, Joseph and Mary probably took the babe there for the ceremony.[74]

Through the act of circumcision and the ceremony surrounding it the infant Jesus was acknowledged as an Israelite, which represented "voluntary subjection to the conditions of the Law, and acceptance of the obligations, but also of the privileges, of the Covenant between God and Abraham and his seed."[75]

This circumcision ceremony is the first of only four events in Jesus' infancy that we are told about in the scriptures. The second and third events may have occurred at the same time. The Savior was the firstborn son of Mary, and in accordance with the second requirement of the Law (Numbers 18:16), he must be "redeemed" from his required service in the temple. The earliest this redemption could have taken place was thirty-one days after his birth, but it may have been that Mary waited until her purification time was completed before fulfilling the redemption requirement.

In order for the child to be redeemed from temple service neither the father nor the mother could be of Levitical descent, and the firstborn son was required to be free from any and all bodily blemishes that would have disqualified him from normal priesthood service.[76] Again, temple attendance was not required, for any priest could have performed the redemption ceremony. To be redeemed from temple service required a payment of five temple shekels (less if the family was poor)[77] in compliance with the Law of Moses (Exodus 13:13; 34:20; Numbers 18:15–16).

The third event that took place was Mary's purification (Leviticus 12:4). The Law required that forty-one days must lapse after the birth of a son before purification could take place. The period was eighty-one days after the birth of a daughter.[78] The purification ceremony could be delayed until a later time on any of the feast days, and the mother was not required to attend the temple. But Mary, a devout Jewess, attended the temple for her purification and took her son with her to be redeemed.[79]

The service was considered a statutory sacrifice, and the legal purification was performed in the court of the women soon after the morning incense had been offered.[80] The sacrifice consisted of presenting two offerings to the Lord. Normally this consisted of a yearling lamb as the burnt offering and a young pigeon or turtledove as the sin offering, both of which were required by the Law (Leviticus 12:1–8; Numbers 18:16). Although Joseph was a carpenter by trade, the offerings presented by Mary were those that the poor could offer in substitution for the more costly offerings. Mary's offerings consisted of two turtledoves or two young pigeons, which again the Law allowed (Leviticus 12:6–8).

The offerings probably were purchased in the yard areas around the temple courts. To ensure that the public did not notice whether the offerings were the normal animals or the less expensive ones, the purchase money was deposited in the appropriate trumpet-shaped chest in the treasury (where the thirteen chests stood for contributions in the Court of the Women).[81] The priests then made the sacrifices, not knowing who the sacrifices belonged to and thus ensuring anonymity and sparing possible embarrassment to the person offering the sacrifice.

Once the ceremony commenced (but before the offering was completed), the participants for purification were found in the court of the women praying to God for their recovery. "After a time, a priest came with some of the blood [of the offering], and, having sprinkled them with it, pronounced them clean, and thus the rite ended."[82] Mary was now Levitically clean and could partake of sacred offerings.[83]

Simeon and Anna

Luke 2:25–38

25. And, behold, there was a man in Jerusalem, whose name was Simeon; and the same man was just and devout, waiting for the consolation of Israel: and the Holy Ghost was upon him.

26. And it was revealed unto him by the Holy Ghost, that he should not see death, before he had seen the Lord's Christ.

27. And he came by the Spirit into the temple: and when the parents brought in the child Jesus, to do for him after the custom of the law,

28. Then took he him up in his arms, and blessed God, and said,

29. Lord, now lettest thou thy servant depart in peace, according to thy word:

30. For mine eyes have seen thy salvation,

31. Which thou hast prepared before the face of all people;

32. A light to lighten the Gentiles, and the glory of thy people Israel.

33. And Joseph and his mother marvelled at those things which were spoken of him.

34. And Simeon blessed them, and said unto Mary his mother, Behold, this child is set for the fall and rising again of many in Israel; and for a sign which shall be spoken against;

35. (Yea, a sword shall pierce through thy own soul also,) that the thoughts of many hearts may be revealed.

36. And there was one Anna, a prophetess, the daughter of Phanuel, of the tribe of Aser: she was of a great age, and had lived with an husband seven years from her virginity;

37. And she was a widow of about fourscore and four years, which departed not from the temple, but served God with fastings and prayers night and day.

38. And she coming in that instant gave thanks likewise unto the Lord, and spake of him to all them that looked for redemption in Jerusalem.

The fourth event described in Jesus' infancy also took place during Mary's purification and her babe's redemption. Simeon, who had been prompted by the Spirit to come to the temple (Luke 2:25–27), met Joseph and Mary there. The New Testament records no prior history for Simeon. We know only that he was an old and devout man who had been promised by the Spirit that he would not die until he had seen the Savior of the world. His heart's longing was now fulfilled, and he recognized in the baby Jesus the long-awaited Messiah. Taking the child in his arms, he broke into song and prophesied.

He first praised God and gave thanks for the fulfillment of his promised blessing. He praised Christ as "a light to lighten the Gentiles, and the glory of thy people Israel" (Luke 2:32), which indicated that he had a correct understanding of the Messiah's future mission and did not totally subscribe to the contemporary Judaic belief.[84] His appearance and actions filled Joseph and Mary with wonder, and they marvelled at his words. Simeon next blessed Mary and Joseph, then he continued to prophesy that Jesus was the stone, the foundation, and the cornerstone upon which all would fall or rise up (Isaiah 8:14).[85] He closed his marvelous interruption of their temple visit with the promise that the Savior's mission would cause deep sorrow in Mary's heart.

Luke (who undoubtedly received his information from Mary)[86] records that upon the completion of Simeon's praise, a woman named Anna appeared, a prophetess of the tribe of Asher. She had been a widow for many years. Because her tribal genealogy had been preserved (even though her tribe was numbered among those that were lost), she apparently came from a family of some distinction.[87]

It seems probable that Anna, like Simeon, had been promised that she would see and recognize the "redemption" of Israel. The scriptures note that she had spent many long years in the temple fasting, praying, and awaiting that redemption. Mary and Joseph may have marvelled at Anna's testimony as they had Simeon's, but the scriptures are silent on their reaction. Their wonder concerning their child only emphasized the fact that they did not yet understand "the magnitude and glory of his mortal ministry and the greatness of the work he would do among men"—although such would "dawn upon them gradually."[88]

With the conclusion of the stories of Simeon and Anna, Luke's description of Christ's infancy ends.

The Magi and Herod the Great

Matthew 2:1-23

1. Now when Jesus was born in Bethlehem of Judaea in the days of Herod the king, behold, there came wise men from the east to Jerusalem,

2. Saying, Where is he that is born King of the Jews? for we have seen his star in the east, and are come to worship him.

3. When Herod the king had heard these things, he was troubled, and all Jerusalem with him.

4. And when he had gathered all the chief priests and scribes of the people together, he demanded of them where Christ should be born.

5. And they said unto him, In Bethlehem of Judaea: for thus it is written by the prophet,

6. And thou Bethlehem, in the land of Juda, art not the least among the princes of Juda: for out of thee shall come a Governor, that shall rule my people Israel.

7. Then Herod, when he had privily called the wise men, enquired of them dili-

gently what time the star appeared.

8. And he sent them to Bethlehem, and said, Go and search diligently for the young child; and when ye have found him, bring me word again, that I may come and worship him also.

9. When they had heard the king, they departed; and, lo, the star, which they saw in the east, went before them, till it came and stood over where the young child was.

10. When they saw the star, they rejoiced with exceeding great joy.

11. And when they were come into the house, they saw the young child with Mary his mother, and fell down, and worshipped him: and when they had opened their treasures, they presented unto him gifts; gold, and frankincense, and myrrh.

12. And being warned of God in a dream that they should not return to Herod, they departed into their own country another way.

13. And when they were departed, behold, the angel of the Lord appeareth to Joseph in a dream, saying, Arise, and take the young child and his mother, and flee into Egypt, and be thou there until I bring thee word: for Herod will seek the young child to destroy him.

14. When he arose, he took the young child and his mother by night, and departed into Egypt:

15. And was there until the death of Herod: that it might be fulfilled which was spoken of the Lord by the prophet, saying, Out of Egypt have I called my son.

16. Then Herod, when he saw that he was mocked of the wise men, was exceeding wroth, and sent forth, and slew all the children that were in Bethlehem, and in all the coasts thereof, from two years old and under, according to the time which he had diligently enquired of the wise men.

17. Then was fulfilled that which was spoken by Jeremy the prophet, saying,

18. In Rama was there a voice heard, lamentation, and weeping, and great mourning, Rachel weeping for her children, and would not be comforted, because they are not.

19. But when Herod was dead, behold, an angel of the Lord appeareth in a dream to Joseph in Egypt,

20. Saying, Arise, and take the young child and his mother, and go into the land of Israel: for they are dead which sought the young child's life.

21. And he arose, and took the young child and his mother, and came into the land of Israel.

22. But when he heard that Archelaus did reign in Judaea in the room of his father Herod, he was afraid to go thither: notwithstanding, being warned of God in a dream, he turned aside into the parts of Galilee:

23. And he came and dwelt in a city called Nazareth: that it might be fulfilled which was spoken by the prophets, He shall be called a Nazarene.

While Luke recorded Israel's homage to the Messiah through his description of the early events in Jesus' life, Matthew recorded the homage of the Gentiles through the visit of the magi. As in

Luke, Matthew records no specific time concerning the visit of the magi (or wise men), but by the time of their visit, Joseph and Mary undoubtedly were no longer living in the cattle stable and had probably moved into a home in Bethlehem.[89]

The descriptive word *magi* (identified in the King James Version of the Bible as "wise men") was a common word at the time the Savior was born and had been used in the Septuagint and later by Josephus both in an evil and in a good sense.[90]

In its evil sense it denoted persons who practiced magical arts, whereas the good sense generally referred to the eastern priest-sages (especially Chaldean) who were revered as having deep knowledge and understanding (even though their knowledge was tinged with superstition).[91] *Magi* may also have referred to a sect of Median and Persian scholars[92] or to pretended astrologers or soothsayers.

The exact number of magi described in the New Testament story cannot be ascertained, but is generally thought of as being three from the number of gifts presented to the Christ child.

The magi began their journey to visit the newborn king because they saw a new star in the heavens. This sign had also been prophesied in the Western Hemisphere (Helaman 14:5). The star appeared at some time after the night without darkness that also occurred at the Savior's birth (3 Nephi 1:21). Likewise, there is no evidence in the New Testament as to when the star first appeared in the heavens, but only that the magi, upon their arrival in Jerusalem, asked Herod, "Where is he that is born King of the Jews? for we have seen his star in the east, and are come to worship him" (Matthew 2:2; see also Numbers 24:17).

They came from an unknown origin in the east. How long they traveled to arrive at Jerusalem is also not known. They had witnessed the new star in the heavens and had regarded that star as a token of the birth of the Messiah who would be the King of the Jews.[93]

They may have begun their journey prior to the Savior's advent so that they could arrive shortly after his birth. However, the star may have appeared at the same time as the Savior's birth, which would result in a later arrival of the magi.[94] Whichever the case, upon their arrival in Jerusalem they immediately went to Herod's palace to gain information about him whom they sought.[95] In their simplicity, they inquired of the leader of the nation that in their understanding the new king would eventually rule. Although Herod was king in Israel and sat upon the throne of David he was not of the Davidic lineage, but was a descendant of Ishmael through Esau and an Idumaean by birth.[96]

Herod received the magi courteously even though the information they presented to him must have filled him with great suspicion and apprehension, for the new king presented a danger to his rule and throne.[97] The magi's inquiry was made known throughout Jerusalem, and the scriptures report that the people were "troubled," perhaps concerning the report of the newborn king but more likely from their fear of Herod's reaction to another claim to the throne of David.[98]

Herod reacted to the magi's questions with his usual cunning and called a council of the priests and scribes. He did not inform them that their anticipated Messiah had already been born, but merely inquired of them where the birthplace would be.

At the time of Herod, the general opinion was that Bethlehem would be the Messiah's birthplace (Micah 5:2),[99] so Herod directed the magi to that city. He asked them to return and tell him of their discovery so that he also might pay homage to the newborn king. Finally, he inquired when the magi had first seen the new star (Matthew 2:7).

After they departed from Herod the star again appeared and the magi rejoiced at seeing it, for apparently they had not seen it for some time.[100] Certainly they did not need the star to direct them to Bethlehem, so it would seem that the star appeared as a testimony to them that Bethlehem was indeed the birthplace of the king they sought.[101] The star seemed to move before them until "it stood over where the young child was—that is, of course, over Bethlehem, not over any special house in it."[102]

Once in Bethlehem they discovered the location of the infant king, but no information is given as to how this was accomplished. The scriptures give no detail concerning the magi's visit to the Savior other than that they paid homage by worshipping him and giving him the gifts of gold, frankincense, and myrrh.[103]

Herod had requested that the magi return and tell him of the location of the new king of the Jews, but because his intentions were evil the magi were warned in a dream not to return to Herod and left instead for their own country. They had come out of scriptural obscurity for their brief visit, and they returned to it after the visit was completed.

When Herod realized that the magi had departed without returning to him he became "exceedingly wroth." Their arrival and their story of the newborn king gave Herod a fresh cause for jealousy and terror. He wanted to kill the child as he had killed others who were a threat to his throne, for Herod's rule had continuously been one of revolting cruelty and unbridled oppression.[104]

With the departure of the magi, Herod had no means of identifying the infant child or of learning his exact birth date, but he was determined to slay this pretender to the throne. Left to his own cunning and based upon his conversation with the wise men, Herod approximated when Jesus must have been born (perhaps taking into account the customary time for the weaning of a child, normally done at two years of age).[105] To ensure the death of the newborn king, the ruthless tyrant gave the order to indiscriminately slaughter all male infants in Bethlehem and its immediate neighborhood under the age of two.

No detail on the means of carrying out the order is given, and perhaps twenty children at most were killed,[106] but the action was in accord with Herod's general character and fulfilled the pain and suffering prophesied of in the Old Testament (Jeremiah 31:15). Herod died within a few days of the slaughtering of the infants,[107] but his descendants to the third generation continued to persecute Christ and shed the blood of his witnesses.[108] Within a hundred years from his death, there were no descendants of Herod the Great left.[109]

To prevent the slaughter of the infant Savior, Joseph had been warned in a dream to take the child and his mother and flee into Egypt. How long they spent in Egypt is unknown —it is only noted that they did not return until after Herod's death.

When they again returned to the land of Israel they intended to stop and make their home in Bethlehem, but again Joseph was warned in a dream that the evil son of Herod, Archelaus, ruled in Judea; so he turned aside and returned to Galilee and Nazareth. There, in remote obscurity, sheltered by apparent insignificance, the Savior of the world began his childhood.

After the return from Egypt and up to the time the Savior was twelve years of age, the scriptures are devoid of any detail concerning his life, except for one verse: "And the child grew, and waxed strong in spirit, filled with wisdom: and the grace of God was upon him" (Luke 2:40).

Childhood

As little as there is recorded of the infancy of Jesus, there is nothing recorded of his childhood. From infancy to twelve years of age we have only the one verse just cited. At twelve we have the incident of his teaching in the temple, which we shall review momentarily, but from that incident until the Savior's entry into his ministry the scriptures only state that he "increased in wisdom and stature, and in favour with God and man" (Luke 2:52).

The silence of the Gospel writers "teaches us once more, and most impressively, that the Gospels furnish a history of the Saviour, not a biography of Jesus of Nazareth."[110] The almost unbroken silence of the scriptures increases rather than gratifies our curiosity, for it furnishes us with no details of his life nor incidence of his adventures. Yet it is evident from what we do know that he was subject to the normal and natural development of all humans.[111] He was born as all humans are born, a helpless child; his infancy undoubtedly contained experiences common to other babies, and his boyhood was probably a natural boyhood. The veil of forgetfulness is common to all, and he undoubtedly developed, as all children develop, from grace to grace, except for the fact that he was not retarded by the weight of sin.[112]

Jesus undoubtedly was raised in the same manner as were other children in his community. As to that, "from the first days of [his] existence, a religious atmosphere surrounded the child of Jewish parents."[113] According to Jewish tradition a child was first educated by the mother, but the primary responsibility for education was the father's, as directed by the Law. (See Deuteronomy 6:7; 11:19; 49:10; Psalm 78:5-6.) In a spiritual and obedient Jewish family, no opportunity was lost to teach religious duty, whether in the morning or evening, at the meal table, at home, or abroad. Every opportunity was taken for "instilling reverence for God's Law into the minds of the family, and of teaching them its express words throughout, till they knew them by heart."[114]

Starting from the fifth or sixth year children were sent to school, where "roughly classifying the subjects of study up to ten years of age, the Bible exclusively should be the text-book; from ten to fifteen, the Mishnah, or traditional law; after that age, the student should enter on those theological discussions which occupied time and attention in the higher Academies of the Rabbis."[115] Christ's early childhood probably was quiet, simple, and uneventful, his life in Nazareth being occupied by home and duties[116] and his obscurity being similar to that of Moses in the wilderness of Midian (Exodus 2:15), David tending his father's sheep (1 Samuel 16:11), Elijah before his showing to Israel (1 Kings 17:1), and Jeremiah in his home in Anathoth (Jeremiah 1:1). The obscurity of his divinity in his early years was later testified to, the scriptures noting that the people of Nazareth felt he was one of them, for they knew his mother, sisters, and brethren (Matthew 13:55-56).

As a child he would have attended the synagogue, for no Israelite would have thought of neglecting those services. There "He came in contact with the religious life of His Race, in its manifold aspects."[117] Paul later described the anonymity of the Savior by stating that he "made himself of no reputation, and took upon him the form of a servant" (Philippians 2:7; see also Isaiah 53:2). While it is evident that the young Jesus was well taught in Jewish society and fully trained in the skills of carpentry, it must be remembered that he was the giver of the Law he studied and was Jehovah incarnate. As he advanced from grace to grace his understanding of his mission and power came direct from his Father.

In the Temple at Twelve

Luke 2:41-51

41. Now his parents went to Jerusalem every year at the feast of the passover.

42. And when he was twelve years old, they went up to Jerusalem after the custom of the feast.

43. And when they had fulfilled the days, as they returned, the child Jesus tarried behind in Jerusalem; and Joseph and his mother knew not of it.

44. But they, supposing him to have been in the company, went a day's journey;

and they sought him among their kinsfolk and acquaintance.

45. And when they found him not, they turned back again to Jerusalem, seeking him.

46. And it came to pass, that after three days they found him in the temple, sitting in the midst of the doctors, both hearing them, and asking them questions.

47. And all that heard him were astonished at his understanding and answers.

48. And when they saw him, they were amazed: and his mother said unto him,

Son, why hast thou thus dealt with us? behold, thy father and I have sought thee sorrowing.

49. And he said unto them, How is it that ye sought me? wist ye not that I must be about my Father's business?

50. And they understood not the saying which he spake unto them.

51. And he went down with them, and came to Nazareth, and was subject unto them: but his mother kept all these sayings in her heart.

The scriptural silence on the Savior's early life is briefly broken by the occasion when, at the age of twelve, the Lord of the temple visited the temple of the Lord. It may not have been his first childhood visit to the temple, but it is the only visit of record during those years, and it occurred as a result of the legal requirements of the Law of Moses. Although thirteen was the legal age when the Law of Moses became binding upon Jewish youth, it was usually anticipated by one or two years.[118]

Thirteen was an important age in Judaism. A young man then commenced learning a trade, and he could no longer be sold as a slave. It was believed that at this age he began to acquire the Spirit. He began wearing a phylactery and was considered a "son of the Law"—or an adult.[119]

The reason for this visit to Jerusalem was the Feast of the Passover. The scriptures note that Christ's earthly parents had gone up every year to this feast as required by the Mosaic Law, but apparently they had not previously taken Jesus. The scriptures offer no detail of the family's activities during the feast days. After the celebration concluded, Joseph and Mary left for Nazareth, but Jesus "tarried behind in Jerusalem."

Joseph and Mary thought he was among the company of kinfolk they were traveling with and did not notice that he was missing until they had traveled a day's journey. Upon discovering his absence they returned to the holy city and searched for him for three days, finally finding him in the temple discussing the doctrines of the Law with the learned.

It was not unusual for a boy of his age to be questioned and to answer questions in the manner the scriptural record describes.[120] There is no record of the questions asked him or the answers he gave, nor of his questions to the doctors of the Law and their answers. All we know is that all who heard him were amazed at his understanding and comprehension of the Law.

Undoubtedly distraught, Mary asked Jesus why he had stayed in the city without telling them, and commented, "Thy father and I have sought thee sorrowing." But Joseph was not the boy's father, and it would seem that he and Mary were momentarily unmindful of the miracle of the child's birth.[121] Perhaps they neither understood nor comprehended the greatness of his mission, and "at times . . . seemingly lost sight of [his] exalted personality."[122] Jesus quickly reminded Mary who he was. "How is it that ye sought me?" He responded. "Wist ye not that I must be about my Father's business?" Clearly Jesus knew who he was even at this tender age.

Jesus had been officially brought to the temple by Joseph and Mary and for the first time, in accordance with Jewish tradition, had had the opportunity to teach and to question. He had been completely engrossed in his conversation with the doctors of the Law, and seemingly unconcerned about his earthly parents' whereabouts. While others did not recognize who he was, and while Joseph and Mary seemed not to have understood the importance of the moment, *he knew.* Yet because he was twelve and still in his childhood, he submitted to the authority of his earthly parents and returned to his home in Nazareth.[123]

Part Two

The Ministry Begins

The
Forerunner

The Messiah whom John the Baptist proclaimed declared his greatness among prophets (Matthew 11:11). John was baptized while yet in his youth and ordained while only eight days of age. His mission was threefold:

1. "To overthrow the kingdom of the Jews."
2. "To make straight the way of the Lord."
3. "To prepare [the people] for the coming of the Lord." (D&C 84:28.)

He was not to be called Zacharias after his father, as was the custom of the day; rather, his name would be John. He became known throughout history as John the Baptist, the forerunner of the Savior of the world.

The Announcement and Birth

Luke 1:5–25, 57–79

5. There was in the days of Herod, the king of Judaea, a certain priest named Zacharias, of the course of Abia: and his wife was of the daughters of Aaron, and her name was Elisabeth.

6. And they were both

righteous before God, walking in all the commandments and ordinances of the Lord blameless.

7. And they had no child, because that Elisabeth was barren, and they both were now well stricken in years.

8. And it came to pass, that while he executed the priest's office before God in the order of his course,

9. According to the custom of the priest's office, his lot was to burn incense when he went into the temple of the Lord.

10. And the whole multitude of the people were praying without at the time of incense.

11. And there appeared unto him an angel of the Lord standing on the right side of the altar of incense.

12. And when Zacharias saw him, he was troubled, and fear fell upon him.

13. But the angel said unto him, Fear not, Zacharias: for thy prayer is heard; and thy wife Elisabeth shall bear thee a son, and thou shalt call his name John.

14. And thou shalt have joy and gladness; and many shall rejoice at his birth.

15. For he shall be great in the sight of the Lord, and shall drink neither wine nor strong drink; and he shall be filled with the Holy Ghost, even from his mother's womb.

16. And many of the children of Israel shall he turn to the Lord their God.

17. And he shall go before him in the spirit and power of Elias, to turn the hearts of the fathers to the children, and the disobedient to the wisdom of the just; to make ready a people prepared for the Lord.

18. And Zacharias said unto the angel, Whereby shall I know this? for I am an old man, and my wife well stricken in years.

19. And the angel answering said unto him, I am Gabriel, that stand in the presence of God; and am sent to speak unto thee, and to shew thee these glad tidings.

20. And, behold, thou shalt be dumb, and not able to speak, until the day that these things shall be performed, because thou believest not my words, which shall be fulfilled in their season.

21. And the people waited for Zacharias, and marvelled that he tarried so long in the temple.

22. And when he came out, he could not speak unto them: and they perceived that

he had seen a vision in the temple: for he beckoned unto them, and remained speechless.

23. And it came to pass, that, as soon as the days of his ministration were accomplished, he departed to his own house.

24. And after those days his wife Elisabeth conceived, and hid herself five months, saying,

25. Thus hath the Lord dealt with me in the days wherein he looked on me, to take away my reproach among men.

57. Now Elisabeth's full time came that she should be delivered; and she brought forth a son.

58. And her neighbours and her cousins heard how the Lord had shewed great mercy upon her; and they rejoiced with her.

59. And it came to pass, that on the eighth day they came to circumcise the child; and they called him Zacharias, after the name of his father.

60. And his mother answered and said, Not so; but he shall be called John.

61. And they said unto her, There is none of thy kindred that is called by this name.

62. And they made signs to his father, how he would have him called.

63. And he asked for a writing table, and wrote, saying, His name is John. And they marvelled all.

64. And his mouth was opened immediately, and his tongue loosed, and he spake, and praised God.

65. And fear came on all that dwelt round about them: and all these sayings were noised abroad throughout all the hill country of Judaea.

66. And all they that heard them laid them up in their hearts, saying, What manner of child shall this be! And the hand of the Lord was with him.

67. And his father Zacharias was filled with the Holy Ghost, and prophesied, saying,

68. Blessed be the Lord God of Israel; for he hath visited and redeemed his people,

69. And hath raised up an horn of salvation for us in the house of his servant David;

70. As he spake by the mouth of his holy prophets, which have been since the world began:

71. That we should be saved from our enemies, and from the hand of all that hate us;

72. To perform the mercy promised to our fathers, and to remember his holy covenant;

73. The oath which he swear to our father Abraham,

74. That he would grant unto us, that we being delivered out of the hand of our enemies might serve him without fear,

75. In holiness and righteousness before him, all the days of our life.

76. And thou, child, shalt be called the prophet of the Highest: for thou shalt go before the face of the Lord to prepare his ways;

77. To give knowledge of salvation unto his people by the remission of their sins,

78. Through the tender mercy of our God; whereby the dayspring from on high hath visited us,

79. To give light to them that sit in darkness and in the shadow of death, to guide our feet into the way of peace.

Cross-references

Luke 1:36, 41–42   Matthew 17:10–13
Mark 9:11–13

Zacharias was an officiating priest in the temple of the Lord in Jerusalem, "of the course of Abia." Originally, King David had divided the temple service of the priesthood into "twenty-four courses" (1 Chronicles 24:1–19), each to serve two one-week periods during the year. The original courses were made up of the descendants of Aaron and the males of the tribe of Levi. However, after the Babylonian captivity only three, or at the most four, of the original courses had returned to the land of promise. Although the original arrangement and names of the courses had been preserved, the membership of the twenty-four courses were now made up by lot from those who had returned to Palestine.[1]

Luke tells us that both Zacharias and his wife, Elisabeth, were well stricken in years. In accordance with Jewish tradition this would have placed them in excess of sixty years of age.[2] They lived in an unknown small town in the hill country of Judea south of Jerusalem. Twice each year, for one week Zacharias would leave his home and come to Jerusalem to perform his priestly duties in the temple.

The scriptures note that Zacharias was a priest and that Elisabeth, his wife, was a daughter of Aaron, and therefore the daughter of a priest.[3] Luke specifically mentions that Zacharias and Elisabeth were childless, from the angel's comment we can conclude that they had prayed for many years to receive the blessing of children. But they were now well stricken in years, and the time had long since passed when the anticipation of a child was on their minds and in their prayers. Yet they are specifically identified as righteous individuals: Luke undoubtedly notes this because of the Jewish tradition that to be childless was a punishment of God.

Generally speaking, the religion of Rabbinism during this time was narrow-minded, bigoted, without spirituality, and mainly concerned with self-aggrandizement.[4] The quiet home where Zacharias and Elisabeth lived was obviously quite different, for they certainly represented "all that was beautiful in the religion of the time."[5]

While ministering during his weekly assignment, Zacharias had been chosen by lot[6] to offer the incense in the temple service. The incense "symbolized Israel's accepted prayers" by God.[7] This privilege usually fell upon a ministering priest only once in his lifetime.[8]

As the worship service of the day progressed, the time came for Zacharias to enter the holy place and stand alone with the golden censer in the glow of the seven-branched candlestick before the veil of the holy of holies.[9] While Zacharias moved to the place that the Jews felt approached "the immediate Presence of God,"[10] the multitude attending the service within the temple courts stood praying, awaiting the time of the incense.[11] Suddenly an angel of the Lord appeared on the right side of the altar of incense before Zacharias. There was no traditional report of such a vision occurring previously to an ordinary priest. The scriptures note that Zacharias was troubled and fearful.

Normally a signal would have been given to notify Zacharias that he should spread the incense upon the altar, entreating the Lord in praise and prayer in behalf of the children of Israel. After spreading the incense, he would have bowed down in worship, then reverently withdrawn. Perhaps the angel appeared before he spread the incense, causing Zacharias to pause in the ceremony. The angel immediately called him by name and announced that his wife, long since barren, would give birth to a son, and that his name should be called John. The blessing many times prayed for (and perhaps long considered impossible) would now be granted to this righteous couple.

The circumstances surrounding the blessing were not unprecedented. Sarah had given birth to a promised child in her later years when both husband and wife felt that childbearing years were over (Genesis 17:17-19; 18:12, 15; JST, Genesis 17:23). Hannah had borne Samuel, and Manoah's wife Samson, after years of barrenness (1 Samuel 1:1-20; Judges 13:1-24).

Zacharias, startled, questioned the angel and asked for a sign that would confirm the angel's promise. The angel, announcing himself as Gabriel, told Zacharias that he would be "dumb" from that time forward, unable to speak because of his doubt.[12] The promised son was to be a special son —full of the Holy Ghost and coming in the spirit and power of Elias to prepare the way before the long-awaited Messiah. The child was to "drink neither wine nor strong drink": he would live the life of a Nazarite, as Samson and Samuel of old had done.

The angel's appearance and his startling message overwhelmed the aged Zacharias, and he tarried long beyond the time when he should have finished the ceremony. The people attending the service waited for him and marvelled that he was so long in the temple.

Zacharias emerged from the holy place and took his position at the top of the steps leading from the porch to the Court of the Priests. Here he should have completed his priestly duties in the service by pronouncing the "benediction, that preceded the daily meat-offering and the chant of the Psalms of praise, accompanied with joyous sound of music, as the drink-offering was poured out."[13] But he could not speak, and while his muteness was a penalty for doubt,[14] by his silence the people knew that a vision had occurred in the temple. No further detail is given. The scriptures merely state that Zacharias finished his ministry in the temple and returned to his wife, Elisabeth, and she conceived to bear a son.

Elisabeth hid herself during the first five months of her pregnancy. During the sixth month, the angel Gabriel appeared to Mary and told her that she had been chosen to be the mother of the Savior of the world. He also told her that Elisabeth had "conceived a son in her old age." After Gabriel departed, Mary left her home in Nazareth and went to visit her cousin Elisabeth, and upon her arrival the unborn John joyfully acknowledged the presence of his Savior when he "leaped" in Elisabeth's womb. Mary remained with Elisabeth until her cousin's delivery drew near, then she returned to her home in Nazareth.

As John's birth approached, the neighbors and family of both Elisabeth and Zacharias rejoiced with her because of the mercy that the Lord had shown her. Eight days after his birth the child was taken for circumcision and naming, as the Jewish law required. Those performing the ceremony wanted to call the newborn son Zacharias, after his father. Elisabeth said no, indicating that the child was to be called John, even though no one in her family was known by that name. Zacharias still could not speak. Those performing the ceremony made signs to him to confirm how the child should be named. Asking for a writing table he wrote, "His name is John." At this moment the penalty for his doubt was lifted and his mouth was opened. His final words nine months before had been words of doubt and fear; now he spoke words of praise to God for granting him such favor.

The births of John and Jesus were both miraculous, and both were announced by the same heavenly messenger. While Gabriel's visit to Mary and the dream of Joseph were known to but few, the visitation of Gabriel to Zacharias and the ensuing birth of John were noised about all the hill country of Judea. Presumably, then, the people, from the lowly peasant up to the mighty Herod (the usurper of the throne), pondered the meaning of the birth of such a child.

With John's birth, the silence of Zacharias was broken and, being filled with the Holy Ghost, he prophesied of his miraculous son's mission. The God of Israel had truly visited his people and had raised up a prophet to prepare the way of the Lord by giving knowledge to his people and spreading light where there had long been darkness.

Nothing is known of John's childhood; however, we must assume that when Herod sent forth his edict to destroy the young children in an attempt to kill the Messiah, John (being only six months older than Jesus) fell under the same condemnation.

Zacharias must have been warned of the coming destruction just as Joseph was, for he "caused [John's] mother to take him into the mountains, where he was raised on locusts and wild honey." Unlike the birth of Jesus, John's birth was public knowledge and the officials questioned Zacharias as to John's whereabouts. But Zacharias "refused to disclose his hiding place, and being the officiating high priest at the Temple that year, [he] was slain by Herod's order, between the porch and the altar."[15]

What occurred during John's long, desert years of seclusion is unknown, and no mention is made in scripture whether Elisabeth, already stricken in years when he was born, lived to rear him to adulthood. The scriptures simply state, "And the child grew, and waxed strong in spirit, and was in the deserts till the day of his shewing unto Israel" (Luke 1:80).

A Voice in the Wilderness

Matthew 3:1–12

1. In those days came John the Baptist, preaching in the wilderness of Judaea,

2. And saying, Repent ye: for the kingdom of heaven is at hand.

3. For this is he that was spoken of by the prophet Esaias, saying, The voice of one crying in the wilderness, Prepare ye the way of the Lord, make his paths straight.

4. And the same John had his raiment of camel's hair, and a leathern girdle about his loins; and his meat was locusts and wild honey.

5. Then went out to him Jerusalem, and all Judaea, and all the region round about Jordan,

6. And were baptized of him in Jordan, confessing their sins.

7. But when he saw many of the Pharisees and Sadducees come to his baptism, he said unto them, O generation of vipers, who hath warned you to flee from the wrath to come?

8. Bring forth therefore fruits meet for repentance:

9. And think not to say within yourselves, We have Abraham to our father: for I say unto you, that God is able of these stones to raise up children unto Abraham.

10. And now also the axe is laid unto the root of the trees: therefore every tree

which bringeth not forth good fruit is hewn down, and cast into the fire.

11. I indeed baptize you with water unto repentance: but he that cometh after me is mightier than I, whose shoes I am not worthy to bear: he shall baptize you with the Holy Ghost, and with fire:

12. Whose fan is in his hand, and he will throughly purge his floor, and gather his wheat into the garner; but he will burn up the chaff with unquenchable fire.

John 1:6–13, 15, 19–28

6. There was a man sent from God, whose name was John.

7. The same came for a witness, to bear witness of the Light, that all men through him might believe.

8. He was not that Light, but was sent to bear witness of that Light.

9. That was the true Light, which lighteth every man that cometh into the world.

10. He was in the world, and the world was made by him, and the world knew him not.

11. He came unto his own, and his own received him not.

12. But as many as received him, to them gave he power to become the sons of God, even to them that believe on his name:

13. Which were born, not of blood, nor of the will of the flesh, nor of the will of man, but of God.

15. John bare witness of him, and cried, saying, This was he of whom I spake, He that cometh after me is preferred before me: for he was before me.

19. And this is the record of John, when the Jews sent priests and Levites from Jerusalem to ask him, Who art thou?

20. And he confessed, and denied not; but confessed, I am not the Christ.

21. And they asked him, What then? Art thou Elias? And he saith, I am not. Art thou that prophet? And he answered, No.

22. Then said they unto him, Who art thou? that we may give an answer to them that sent us. What sayest thou of thyself?

23. He said, I am the voice of one crying in the wil-

derness, Make straight the way of the Lord, as said the prophet Esaias.

24. And they which were sent were of the Pharisees.

25. And they asked him, and said unto him, Why baptizest thou then, if thou be not that Christ, nor Elias, neither that prophet?

26. John answered them, saying, I baptize with water: but there standeth one among you, whom ye know not;

27. He it is, who coming after me is preferred before me, whose shoe's latchet I am not worthy to unloose.

28. These things were done in Bethabara beyond Jordan, where John was baptizing.

Cross-references

Mark 1:1–8   Luke 3:1–20

When his time came, John — a student of heavenly teachers[16] like Moses (Exodus 3:1–2) and Elijah (1 Kings 17:2–7), before him, and the herald of the long-awaited Messiah — began his ministry.

He came from the wilderness: his hair long, his beard heavy, his body clothed in a raiment of camel's hair with a leather girdle about his loins. He was like the prophets of old, a reminder of times past (2 Kings 1:8). His appearance was reminiscent of Elijah the Tishbite, "whom all expected to reappear before the Messiah."[17] He fulfilled Isaiah's prophecy, for he was the "voice of him that crieth in the wilderness [saying], Prepare ye the way of the Lord, make straight in the desert a highway for our God" (Isaiah 40:3).

As the forerunner he acted as a hinge between the two testaments. He was the last prophet of the Mosaic Law, "the only legal administrator in the affairs of the kingdom,"[18] and heir of all past ages — transcending all that had gone before while making way for that which was yet to come.

He extolled the Law of Moses, yet was a severe critic of what it had become. He spoke nothing of the rabbis or Levitical rites and sacrifices but demanded a moral conscience from the Jews.[19] He used the ax at the root of the tree (Matthew 3:10) and bore witness against all the evils of his time.

John the Baptist, unlike Jesus, was the prophet of anticipation;[20] the returning Elijah who would "bring back the lost Urim and Thummim, restore the tribes of Israel, turn the hearts of the fathers to the children, reprove the times, and appease the wrath of God."[21] John stirred such deep memories within the multitude and the leadership that they could ignore neither him nor his message.

John's rite of baptism was administered to the truly penitent. Just as Jacob and Moses had attempted to purify all Israel to receive God's presence (Genesis 35:2; Exodus 19:10, 14), so for the same reason those accepting John's baptism sought purification from sins committed under the old Law.

Baptism itself was not new. Under the Law of Moses it symbolically removed the moral defilement that caused Levitical uncleanliness. New proselytes were also baptized as they accepted the Law of Moses.[22] But John's baptism differed substantially from that of his predecessors. *His baptism initiated a turning from the past in anticipation of the future, the coming Christ, and a newness of life.* John was merely the harbinger for the Savior who would come and baptize with fire.

John's emphasis on repentance fit into the accepted teachings of his day, for the Jewish rulers taught that "if Israel repented but one day, the Son of David would immediately come."[23] But while John's demands were full of "promise to the repentant soul, [they were] scathingly denunciatory to the hypocrite and the hardened sinner."[24] He denounced the Pharisees and Sadducees as transgressors of the spirit of the Law, and accused them of dishonoring the prophets.[25] They revelled in the teaching that, because they were the children of Abraham, they were automatically saved in God's kingdom.[26] John chastised them for their belief, requiring them to bring forth fruits meet for repentance and stating that God could "of these stones raise up children unto Abraham." Yet they anticipated, perhaps yearned for, the very one John testified was to come. In their ignorance they sent emissaries to John to ask if he was the Christ. "No," was the swift reply. "What then? Art thou Elias?" "No." John the Baptist was the forerunner, come to "make straight the way of the Lord" in the spirit and power of Elias.[27]

John preached the fundamental principles of the gospel of Jesus Christ: *faith* as a revitalized belief in God; *repentance* as contrition for past offenses; and *baptism* as the symbolistic rite of the fulfill-ment and completion of these doctrines. His teachings were famil-iar to both the Jewish leadership and the multitude, for they had been read and studied for centuries in the synagogues and in the scriptures.[28] Although his sermons frequently opposed the popular practices of his time,[29] the scriptures report that all Jerusalem went out to see him.

John came in the Jewish mode of prophets to raise his nation from spiritual death and direct it towards the Messiah.[30] He pro-fessed no visions or revelations: he performed no miracles. In all that he did he acknowledged the status of his mission, taking nei-ther power nor glory unto himself. "His was not a call to armed re-sistance, but to repentance . . . the hope which he held out was not of earthly possessions, but of purity." He was "unbendingly firm . . . deep [with] settled conviction; not ambitious nor self-seeking . . . discarding all claim but that of lowliest service, and pointing away from himself to Him Who was to come, and Whom as yet he did not even know. . . . For himself he sought nothing . . . he had only one absorbing thought: The Kingdom was at hand, the King was coming —let them prepare!"[31]

The Baptism of Jesus and the Sign of the Dove

Matthew 3:13–17

13. Then cometh Jesus from Galilee to Jordan unto John, to be baptized of him.

14. But John forbad him, saying, I have need to be bap-tized of thee, and comest thou to me?

15. And Jesus answering said unto him, Suffer it to be so now: for thus it becometh us to fulfil all righteousness. Then he suffered him.

16. And Jesus, when he was baptized, went up straightway out of the water: and, lo, the heavens were opened unto him, and he saw the Spirit of God descending like a dove, and lighting upon him:

17. And lo a voice from heaven, saying, This is my beloved Son, in whom I am well pleased.

John 1:29-34

29. The next day John seeth Jesus coming unto him, and saith, Behold the Lamb of God, which taketh away the sin of the world.

30. This is he of whom I said, After me cometh a man which is preferred before me: for he was before me.

31. And I knew him not: but that he should be made manifest to Israel, therefore am I come baptizing with water.

32. And John bare record, saying, I saw the Spirit descending from heaven like a dove, and it abode upon him.

33. And I knew him not: but he that sent me to baptize with water, the same said unto me, Upon whom thou shalt see the Spirit descending, and remaining on him, the same is he which baptizeth with the Holy Ghost.

34. And I saw, and bare record that this is the Son of God.

While John was baptizing in the River Jordan at Bethabara he baptized the Savior.[32] Although Jesus and John were cousins,[33] there is no evidence of any personal contact between them prior to this meeting.[34] However, as soon as John saw the Lord he recognized a sinless man (undoubtedly through the Spirit) and proclaimed his own need to be baptized by Jesus. John's call was to repentance and his baptism was a sign of that repentance, but before him stood one for whom he considered baptism unnecessary.[35] However, baptism was required of the Lord just as it is of all men, and Jesus responded to John's protest by stating that his baptism was necessary "to fulfil all righteousness."

Jesus' baptism was not a sign of repentance but a simple act of submission and obedience, because baptism is "an indispensible ordinance established in righteousness and required of all mankind as an essential condition for membership in the kingdom of God."[36]

John knew before he entered his ministry that he would baptize the Messiah, for he had been given a sign whereby he would recognize him. At the conclusion of the Lord's baptism a "sign" of new life occurred, similar to that previously given to Noah by Jehovah (Genesis 8:10-12). This was the sign of the dove.

The sign of the dove was the "foreappointed means by which the Messiah should be made known to [John],"[37] and it "was instituted before the creation of the world, [as] a witness for the Holy Ghost. . . . [It was] given to John to signify the truth of the deed."[38] At the conclusion of this sacred experience, the voice of the Father was heard testifying to the divinity of His Son. The Messiah was now known to John, and henceforth he would testify that the one he had prepared for had indeed arrived and all should look to Him for salvation.

With Jesus' baptism performed, John's witness given of the coming of the Bridegroom, the sign given, and the Father's testimony pronounced, John's calling was basically fulfilled. His public greatness would now wane as the Lord increased in power and authority (John 3:25-30).

Disciples

John 1:35-37

35. Again the next day after John stood, and two of his disciples;

36. And looking upon Jesus as he walked, he saith,

Behold the Lamb of God!

37. And the two disciples heard him speak, and they followed Jesus.

John 3:23-36

23. And John also was baptizing in Aenon near to Salim, because there was much water there: and they came, and were baptized.

24. For John was not yet cast into prison.

25. Then there arose a question between some of

John's disciples and the Jews about purifying.

26. And they came unto John, and said unto him, Rabbi, he that was with thee beyond Jordan, to whom thou barest witness, behold, the same baptizeth, and all men come to him.

27. John answered and said, A man can receive nothing, except it be given him from heaven.

28. Ye yourselves bear me witness, that I said, I am not the Christ, but that I am sent before him.

29. He that hath the bride is the bridegroom: but the friend of the bridegroom, which standeth and heareth him, rejoiceth greatly because of the bridegroom's voice: this my joy therefore is fulfilled.

30. He must increase, but I must decrease.

31. He that cometh from above is above all: he that is of the earth is earthly, and speaketh of the earth: he that cometh from heaven is above all.

32. And what he hath seen and heard, that he testifieth; and no man receiveth his testimony.

33. He that hath received his testimony hath set to his seal that God is true.

34. For he whom God hath sent speaketh the words of God: for God giveth not the Spirit by measure unto him.

35. The Father loveth the Son, and hath given all things into his hand.

36. He that believeth on the Son hath everlasting life: and he that believeth not the Son shall not see life; but the wrath of God abideth on him.

Initially John's preaching drew many disciples to him, including Andrew and John the Beloved—perhaps also Peter, Philip, and Nathanael—all of whom would later become Apostles of the Lord.[39] His sermons prepared his disciples for belief in Jesus Christ, and it was obviously his intention that his disciples should leave him and move on to the Savior. However, it does not appear that any of John's disciples were formally introduced to the Savior, but rather those that followed him introduced themselves, relying upon John's testimony concerning Jesus.[40]

After the Lord began his mission, John briefly continued his ministry, and many of his disciples stayed with him. Some even became jealous of Jesus' rise and their master's decline.[41] It may have seemed to them that Jesus had snatched away the fruits of John's ministry. In spite of this, John continued to testify of Jesus' rise and of his own decline; however, some of his disciples remained uncertain of their master's proclamation that Jesus was the Christ. The multitudes that had followed John now followed the Lord, and some of John's remaining disciples (perhaps with some animosity) told him of the Lord's success. John's reply reflected his constant acceptance of his own mission as compared with the Messiah's. He again bore witness that Jesus was the Christ and the only one whom they should be following.

On yet another occasion, John's disciples (assisted by the Pharisees, who undoubtedly harbored evil intent) apparently became entangled in a potential controversy with the Lord concerning fasting and prayer. It appears that while John and his disciples fasted often, Jesus' disciples did not fast. Jesus did not dispute this conflict but treated the question as one which required enlightenment rather than argument. Rather than censure John's disciples for fasting, he defended his own followers for not fasting.[42]

Imprisonment and Death

Matthew 14:1–12

1. At that time Herod the tetrach heard of the fame of Jesus,

2. And said unto his servants, This is John the Baptist; he is risen from the dead; and therefore mighty works do shew forth themselves in him.

3. For Herod had laid hold on John, and bound him, and put him in prison for Herodias' sake, his brother Philip's wife.

4. For John said unto him, It is not lawful for thee to have her.

5. And when he would have put him to death, he feared the multitude, because they counted him as a prophet.

6. But when Herod's birthday was kept, the daughter of Herodias danced before them, and pleased Herod.

7. Whereupon he promised with an oath to give her whatsoever she would ask.

8. And she, being before instructed of her mother, said, Give me here John Baptist's head in a charger.

9. And the king was sorry: nevertheless for the oath's sake, and them which sat with him at meat, he commanded it to be given her.

10. And he sent, and beheaded John in the prison.

11. And his head was brought in a charger, and given to the damsel: and she brought it to her mother.

12. And his disciples came, and took up the body, and buried it, and went and told Jesus.

Cross-references

Matthew 11:1–6   Mark 6:14–29

While John was preaching in the territory of Herod Antipas, Herodias convinced Herod to arrest him, for "she had a quarrel against him."[43] Herodias was living with Herod Antipas as his wife, even though she had previously married Herod's brother and had not been lawfully divorced from him —a circumstance which John denounced.

After John was seized by Herod, Jesus withdrew into Galilee (Matthew 4:12), and John commenced his long incarceration in the prison at Machaerus. While the slow months of imprisonment passed, Herod frequently "heard him,"[44] for Herod found him to be a holy man and listened to him gladly.[45] Although Herod seemed fearful of John, clearly his motives for John's imprisonment were political. These political motives could be classified into three general categories: (1) John had a great influence over the people, and Herod feared that this influence might lead to a revolt within the kingdom. (2) The Jewish leadership did not like Herod's marriage to Herodias, and he feared that this dislike, coupled with the denunciations from John, might also lead to rebellion. (3) The Pharisees were constantly watching both John and Jesus, and the inference could be made "that [the] Pharisaic intrigue had a very large share in giving effect to Herod's fear of the Baptist and of his reproofs."[46]

Alfred Edersheim gives us a vivid description of the prison or "keep" into which Herod cast John:

The foundations of the walls all around, to the height of a yard or two above the ground, are still standing. As we clamber over them to examine the interior, we notice how small this keep is: exactly 100 yards in diameter. There is scarcely any remains of it left. A well of great depth, and a deep cemented cistern with the vaulting of the roof still complete, and — of most terrible interest to us — two dungeons, one of them deep down, its sides scarcely broken in, 'with small holes still visible in the masonry where staples of wood and iron had once been fixed'! As we look down into its hot darkness, we shudder in realizing that this terrible keep had for nigh ten months been the prison of that son of the free 'wilderness,' the bold herald of the coming Kingdom, the humble, earnest, self-denying John the Baptist.[47]

Is it any wonder that, as a result of his loneliness and suffering, after months of imprisonment John should send his disciples to the Lord seemingly to ask, "Am I right, or in error?"[48] It would be an injustice to John to say that he doubted the Savior of the world, whom he had baptized, but it would appear that he may not have understood fully the Messiah's mission[49] and needed assurance that the "Mighty One" of Israel had not forgotten him.[50] The Lord's response to John's disciples seems to indicate that this was the case. The Lord asked John's disciples to watch as he performed extensive acts of compassion and mercy, and then to return and tell John what they had seen.[51] After they left, Jesus testified to John's greatness, stating that no greater prophet had been born of woman. It is probably at this time that he sent angels to visit the imprisoned Baptist (JST, Matthew 4:11).

Why did Jesus express himself as he did about John's greatness as a prophet? The Prophet Joseph Smith explained:

The question arose from the saying of Jesus — "Among those that are born of women there is not a greater prophet than John the Baptist; but he that is least in the kingdom of God is greater than he." How is it that John was considered one of the greatest prophets? His miracles could not have constituted his greatness.

First. He was entrusted with the divine mission of preparing the way before the face of the Lord. Whoever had such a trust committed to him before or since? No man.

Secondly. He was entrusted with the important mission, and it was required at his hands, to baptize the Son of Man.

Whoever had the honor of doing that? Whoever had so great a privilege and glory? Whoever led the Son of God into the waters of baptism, and had the privilege of beholding the Holy Ghost descend in the form of a dove, or rather in the *sign* of a dove, in witness of that administration? . . .

Thirdly. John, at that time, was the only legal administrator in the affairs of the kingdom there was then on the earth, and holding the keys of power. The Jews had to obey his instructions or be damned, by their own law; and Christ Himself fulfilled all righteousness in becoming obedient to the law which he had given to Moses on the mount, and thereby magnified it and made it honorable, instead of destroying it. The son of Zacharias wrested the keys, the kingdom, the power, the glory from the Jews, by the holy anointing and decree of heaven, and these three reasons constitute him the greatest prophet born of a woman.[52]

The end was near for John. Early in the spring, but before the Passover, Herod Antipas (the successor to Herod the Great) ordered a feast to celebrate his birthday. As the banquet progressed, the music and shouts of revelry must have filtered into the citadel, echoing into the deep dungeon where John was imprisoned.

The merriment reached great heights of excitement until, as a conclusion to the festivities, a "sensuous stimulus of dubious dances" was presented to the lords, military authorities, and political leaders of Galilee. The dancer was Salome[53] "the fair young daughter of the king's wife, the very descendant of the Asmonean priest-princesses!" She danced her best in that exhibition, pleasing Herod and all those who sat with him. Among the ensuing plaudits, the king swore in the hearing of the whole company that he would reward her with whatever she wanted, "even to the half of his kingdom." According to Mark's account, the maiden retired from the banquet hall to consult with her mother about what gift to ask for. "[Could] there be doubt or hesitation in the mind of Herodias? If there was one object she had at heart, which these ten months she had in vain sought to attain, it was the death of John the Baptist."[54]

John had incessantly condemned her for her adulterous marriage to Herod, and so the boon was conceived and Herodias's daughter made haste to the king and said, "I will that thou give me by and by in a charger the head of John the Baptist!" All in the room must have been shocked at this sadistic request. The scriptures note that "the king was exceeding sorry," but he had sworn to reward the maiden, and although he was being "unfaithful to his God, to his conscience, [and] to truth and righteousness . . . he would yet be faithful to his half-drunken oath, and appear honorable and true before such companions!" Straightway he gave the order. Salome withdrew as the guardsmen left the banquet hall. No time for preparation was given, nor was it needed, for a few moments later the "gory head of the Baptist [was] brought to the maiden in a charger, and she [gave] the ghastly dish to her mother."[55] John the Baptist was dead.

But he was dead only as defined in mortality, and even then for only a few short years while he awaited his glorious resurrection. He would be heard from centuries later when he appeared in all his power on the banks of the Susquehanna River to bestow the priesthood upon two humble servants who had been called to overthrow a different kingdom. With these glorious words John the Baptist restored that same priesthood which he had held: "Upon you my fellow servants, in the name of Messiah I confer the Priesthood of Aaron, which holds the keys of the ministering of angels, and of the gospel of repentance, and of baptism by immersion for the remission of sins; and this shall never be taken again from the earth, until the sons of Levi do offer again an offering unto the Lord in righteousness" (D&C 13).

To Fulfill All Righteousness

4

Baptism

Matthew 3:13-17

13. Then cometh Jesus from Galilee to Jordan unto John, to be baptized of him.

14. But John forbad him, saying, I have need to be baptized of thee, and comest thou to me?

15. And Jesus answering said unto him, Suffer it to be so now: for thus it becometh us to fulfil all righteousness. Then he suffered him.

16. And Jesus, when he was baptized, went up straightway out of the water: and, lo, the heavens were opened unto him, and he saw the Spirit of God descending like a dove, and lighting upon him:

17. And lo a voice from heaven, saying, This is my beloved Son, in whom I am well pleased.

Cross-references

Mark 1:7-11   Luke 3:21-23
John 1:32-34   2 Nephi 31:5-12

Baptism has always been and remains, in Elder James E. Talmage's words, "an indispensable ordinance established in righteousness and required of all mankind as an essential condition for membership in the Kingdom of God."[1] President Lorenzo Snow testified, "There is but one way in which men can receive salvation, exaltation and glory, and that is through the order of baptism and the ordinances connected therewith . . . that is the order that God has established."[2]

Baptism was required from the beginning. Adam was baptized (Moses 6:64–65; see also 1 Corinthians 10:1–4), and Jesus began his public ministry by being baptized "to fulfil all righteousness."

Baptism was recognized and practiced among the Jews at Christ's time,[3] but Jesus specifically sought out John the Baptist to perform His baptism.

John preached the necessity of repentance before baptism in order to receive forgiveness for sin, but the Lord needed neither repentance nor forgiveness. The scriptures make it clear, however, that the Son of God did need the ordinance of baptism. Even the sinless Messiah could not regain the kingdom of the Father without it.

Nephi of old witnessed the baptism of the Savior in vision (1 Nephi 11:27). While teaching of this vision to emphasize the absolute necessity of baptism for all men, he was questioned about the need for the perfect Son to be baptized "to fulfil all righteousness." Understanding the perfection of the Lamb of God before the Father and the fact that he had no need for repentance, Nephi then taught five basic reasons for the Savior's baptism (which also apply to all men):

1. To show "unto the children of men that, according to the flesh he humbleth himself before the Father."

2. To witness "unto the Father that he would be obedient unto him in keeping his commandments."

3. To show that baptism was necessary prior to receiving the Holy Ghost, which, after the Lord's baptism, descended upon him just as it had upon Adam (Moses 6:65).[4]

4. To show "unto the children of men the straightness of the path, and the narrowness of the gate, by which they should enter."

5. To invite all of the children of men to "follow thou me."

Nephi continued this instruction to his brethren by exclaiming, "O then, how much more need have we, being unholy, to be baptized, yea, even by water!" (2 Nephi 31:5-12.)

The scriptures are void of detail concerning the eighteen years between the Savior's appearance at age twelve in the temple and the time of his baptism (Luke 2:52), but the time eventually arrived when he left his protected life in Nazareth and entered the mission for which he had been born — to "be about his Father's business."

When John took the Savior into the waters of the Jordan, he closed the door on Israel's dead past and initiated its future: in a similar sense the Savior's past life was finished, and the new era of his ministry opened before him. The miraculous occurrences that transpired immediately thereafter testify that the Father accepted the Son's obedience, for immediately upon his coming forth out of the water the Holy Ghost descended upon him, as witnessed by the sign of the dove.[5] The descent of the Holy Ghost upon him had been foreseen by Nephi and Isaiah (1 Nephi 11:27; Isaiah 11:2). Thus the prophecies of the Old Testament concerning the commencement of the Lord's ministry were fulfilled.

The baptism of fire by the Holy Ghost was the foreappointed sign by which the Messiah would be made known, and from henceforth "John knew his Redeemer."[6] In addition to this sign (and as if to ratify the mission of the forerunner) the Father opened the heavens and spoke, testifying of his Son's divinity. The Savior's past life was over: with his baptism came a new era and the opening of his public ministry.

Authority and Baptism

For the Savior's baptism to be accepted and recognized in the sight of God, it had to be performed by one holding the proper authority. John had been ordained and given that authority when he was eight days old (D&C 84:28). Paul taught this principle of proper authority when he was instructing certain disciples in Ephesus. Upon questioning them, he discovered that although they had been baptized by "someone," it had been done without the proper authority; he then rebaptized them all (Acts 19:1-6). In the Book of Mormon, King Limhi and many of his people desired baptism, but it was postponed because "there was none in the land that had authority from God" (Mosiah 21:33).

As Joseph Smith was translating the Book of Mormon, he came upon passages concerning the necessity of baptism. Not yet understanding the sacred doctrine, he and Oliver Cowdery, his scribe, went to the Lord in prayer for clarification and received the following answer:

> A messenger from heaven descended in a cloud of light, and having laid his hands upon us, he ordained us saying:
> "Upon you my fellow servants, in the name of Messiah, I confer the Priesthood of Aaron, which holds the keys of the ministering of angels, and of the gospel of repentance, and of baptism by immersion for the remission of sins." . . .
> The messenger who visited us on this occasion and conferred this Priesthood upon us, said that his name was John, the same that is called John the Baptist in the New Testament. (Joseph Smith—History 1:68–69, 72.)

Having received the proper authority and having conferred it upon each other as they were instructed, Joseph and Oliver then baptized each other in the Susquehanna River.

The Covenant

Nephi indicated that in the baptismal covenant each person "witnesseth unto the Father that [he will] be obedient unto him in keeping his commandments" (2 Nephi 31:7).

Paul, writing to the Romans, declared, "Know ye not, that so many of us as were baptized into Jesus Christ were baptized into his death? Therefore we are buried with him by baptism into death." (Romans 6:3–4.) In baptism we symbolically bury our former life and existence and agree to come forth out of the water in the likeness of Christ (as if out of the grave), to "walk in newness of life." Paul continued: "Like as Christ was raised up from the dead by the glory of the Father, even so we also should walk in newness of life. For if we have been planted together in the likeness of his death, we shall be also in the likeness of his resurrection: Knowing this, that our old man is crucified with him, that the body of sin might be destroyed, that henceforth we should not serve sin." Concluding the metaphor, Paul declared, "Let not sin therefore reign in your mortal body." (Romans 6:4–12.)

The "old man" is our past — our sinful nature, the actual commission of sin, the breaking of the Lord's commandments. Paul's similitude of death is the dying of sin: thus we should serve sin no longer; rather, in the likeness of the resurrection of Christ, we are to be alive (acceptable) unto God.

In explaining the baptismal covenant, Paul used this metaphorical teaching in almost all of his epistles.[7] His was a consistent theme of putting off the old ways of the past, rejecting sinful habits, and setting a new course dedicated to righteousness and an absolute struggle for obedience.

The Lord confirmed Paul's teachings in a revelation to Joseph Smith when he explained that "after they are received by baptism. . . . the members shall manifest before the Church, and also before the elders, by a godly walk and conversation, that they are worthy of it [baptism], that there may be works and faith agreeable to the holy scriptures — walking in holiness before the Lord." (D&C 20:68–69.) This is the covenant we make at baptism.

Baptism for the Remission of Sins

The fourth article of faith declares: "We believe that the first principles and ordinances of the Gospel are: first, Faith in the Lord Jesus Christ; second, Repentance; *third, Baptism by immersion for the remission of sins;* fourth, Laying on of hands for the gift of the Holy Ghost" (italics added). The ordinance of baptism does not of itself wash away sin, nor does the *water* remove sin, for if a person enters the waters of baptism filthy and unrepentant he will come out of the water filthy still. How then is baptism performed for the remission of sins?

The scriptures note that John the Baptist "came into all the country about Jordan, preaching the baptism *of repentance* for the remission of sins" (Luke 3:3; italics added). It is repentance that makes possible the remission of sin through the atonement of Jesus Christ. Baptism establishes a covenant between the individual and God and is the symbol of remission. Moroni explains it in this way: "And the first fruits of repentance is baptism; and baptism cometh by faith unto the fulfilling the commandments; and the fulfilling of the commandments bringeth remission of sins" (Moroni 8:25).

Baptism is the sign by which we declare to God our sincere repentance, that we have completely forsaken sin, and that we will henceforth obey all his commandments. Further, it is the sign of God's covenant with us that, providing our repentance is complete, our sins will be remitted.

Temptations

Matthew 4:1–11

1. Then was Jesus led up of the Spirit into the wilderness to be tempted of the devil.

2. And when he had fasted forty days and forty nights, he was afterward an hungred.

3. And when the tempter came to him, he said, If thou be the Son of God, command that these stones be made bread.

4. But he answered and said, It is written, Man shall not live by bread alone, but by every word that proceedeth out of the mouth of God.

5. Then the devil taketh him up into the holy city, and setteth him on a pinnacle of the temple,

6. And saith unto him, If thou be the Son of God, cast thyself down: for it is written, He shall give his angels charge concerning thee: and in their hands they shall bear thee up, lest at any time thou dash thy foot against a stone.

7. Jesus said unto him, It is written again, Thou shalt not tempt the Lord thy God.

8. Again, the devil taketh him up into an exceeding high mountain, and sheweth him all the kingdoms of the world, and the glory of them;

9. And saith unto him, All these things will I give thee, if thou wilt fall down and worship me.

10. Then saith Jesus unto him, Get thee hence, Satan: for it is written, Thou shalt worship the Lord thy God, and him only shalt thou serve.

11. Then the devil leaveth him, and, behold, angels came and ministered unto him.

Cross-references

Mark 1:12–13   Luke 4:1–13

There are some variances in the scriptural histories which relate the events of Christ's temptations. In fact, the Gospel of John begins its historical treatment of Jesus' life after the temptations had occurred. Mark speaks of them in general, agreeing with the narratives of Matthew and Luke that Jesus was led by the Spirit into the wilderness and was with the wild beasts.

Matthew and Luke report the first temptation the same but invert the order of the final two temptations. In Matthew we note that "angels came and ministered unto Jesus" at the conclusion of the temptations, and Luke concludes with the tempter departing from Jesus "for a season." The Gospel of Matthew will be followed in this discussion.

After his baptism, Jesus was led into the wilderness, where he would receive the devil's assaults. For a period of forty days he fasted and prayed. His formal ministry had begun, and he chose to fast at this time so that his mortal body might be made more completely subject to his spirit.[8]

Such a lengthy fast had occurred previously in Israel's history. Both Moses and Elijah had fasted for forty-day periods (Deuteronomy 9:9; 1 Kings 19:8). Moses had fasted in the presence of God, and was given the Covenant so that the children of Israel might obey the Law. After his forty-day fast it was evident that the Israelites had not even obeyed the simple instructions he had given them, so with indignation he cast down and broke the tablets of the Law. Elijah had also attempted to convince the children of Israel to obey the Law and tried to restore God's covenant to them, but he had no greater success than Moses. Like Jesus, the patriarchs and other Israelite leaders had been tried and proven through Satan's assaults.[9] It is interesting to note that one of the questions presented to Jesus was why his disciples did not fast.[10]

The three specific temptations that the Lord endured are generally reported as being the culmination of his forty-day fast. Luke's narrative seems to indicate that Jesus was tempted during the entire forty-day period, but the Joseph Smith Translation clarifies this as being otherwise (JST, Luke 4:2). Further, as the scriptures note, the devil departed from him for a season, but he would return to tempt him at other times and in other ways as opportunity presented itself.[11] Echoes of the three temptations occur throughout the Lord's ministry: his brothers suggested he show himself to the leadership of Israel at Jerusalem (John 7:3-5); there was a popular attempt to make him a political king after the feeding of the five thousand in the wilderness;[12] and Pilate tempted him with the question, "Art thou a king then?" (John 18:37.)

At the conclusion of Christ's wilderness fast, and at a time when he felt the greatest physical weariness and weakness from hunger, Lucifer initiated the three specific temptations. During the preceding days his future work and mission were, in all probability, constantly on his mind. Having spent forty days and forty nights in fasting and prayer, the Master of all that was good would now be confronted by the master of all that was evil. As the great "son of the morning" and deceiver of mankind stood before him, Satan presented his three great temptations, the total experience resolving itself into "one question of absolute submission to the will of God, which is the sum and substance of all obedience."[13]

The Temptations of Jesus

The First Temptation: The scriptures report that Jesus was "an hungered." In this weakened state, Satan came with all his subtlety and cunning, saying, "If thou be the Son of God, command that these stones be made bread."

The reaction of the flesh to such a long fast would typically have been predictable, for the Lord's body hungered for nourishment. He was physically weak, "and this was the tempter's moment. The whole period had been one of moral and spiritual tension . . . [and now was] . . . the hour of extreme danger . . . the moment in which [many men have] fallen a victim to insidious allurement or bold assault. It was at such a moment that the great battle of our Lord against the powers of evil was fought and won."[14]

The temptation was disguised within the need of the moment, and the father of all lies presumptuously thought he had cradled within the guise of food the temptation that would destroy a God. Perhaps Satan thought that Christ, like Esau, would trade away his birthright for food (Genesis 25:33). Was not this Jehovah, he who had provided Hagar with water so that she could save herself and her son from death (Genesis 21:15-19)? Even Israel, while being led out of captivity, had struggled with mass hunger and was fed manna in the wilderness by God (Exodus 16:15). And had not Elijah been shown food by an angel at the time of his need (1 Kings 19:4-8)? So the tempter stood before the Messiah (who would later feed five thousand and more on one occasion and four thousand-plus on another), and tempted the God of creation to yield and create food for himself.

This temptation was not one of mere food, however, for the devil had asked the Savior to do much more than use his supernatural power to gratify his physical need. He had cunningly taunted, "*If* thou be the Son of God . . ." (italics added). Food was not the temptation, but doubt. Satan was asking the Lord to doubt his divine relationship with the Father. He who was born of no earthly father, no natural man, but was eternally endowed with Godhood from birth—the Only Begotten of the Father in the flesh—was now being asked to doubt that relationship. Both the Lord and the devil had a perfect understanding of the point in question, and both knew that to yield was to doubt, and thereby fail.

With a sharp retort the Lord answered: "It is written, man shall not live by bread alone, but by every word that proceedeth out of the mouth of God." The need for physical self-preservation was great, but the Lord's answer dictated that all appetites should be kept within the bounds set by the divine standard. God's word would prevail, not Christ's temporal needs, even though he possessed unlimited power. Only forty days previously the Father had testified of the divinity of his Son, and Jesus easily overcame the first temptation by absolute trust in the Father and submission to His will.

The Second Temptation: In the second temptation the Lord was transported by the Spirit to the holy city of Jerusalem and set upon a pinnacle of the temple (JST, Matthew 4:5). The devil, persistent in his purpose to destroy the Son of God, tempted him there. The Lord had used scripture to close the previous temptation, and the devil now used scripture to open the second one. Again the insidious "if" prefaced his comments, but in the design of this temptation the devil quoted a Messianic prophecy that had to be fulfilled: "He [God] shall give his angels charge concerning thee; and in their hands they shall bear thee up, lest at any time thou dash thy foot against a stone." The evil one was subtly asking the Lord to question the very trust in the Father he had used to overcome the first temptation by wantonly throwing himself into a predicament that would test the Father's promise.

In the first temptation the devil had attempted to create doubt in the Lord's mind concerning his divine sonship, and the implication of doubt was again implied in this temptation. But Satan's ultimate goal was to awaken within the Savior an arrogant pride of his relationship with the Father. It was not just his safety on the pinnacle of the temple that was at stake, but the control of his pride, for this was a temptation of the spirit (Psalm 91:11–12). Satan was appealing to the human side of Christ's nature at this point, tempting him to tempt his Father, for it was not the destruction of the body but the destruction of the Savior's soul that the devil wanted. In response to all this the Savior simply stated, "It is written again, Thou shalt not tempt the Lord thy God."

The Third Temptation: The setting for the final temptation was a high mountaintop, from whence was projected in vision all of the world's riches with its kingdoms and glory. Casting aside all subtlety, the tempter exhibited his own weakness before the Master of good by promising him the kingdoms of the world on the condition that "Thou wilt fall down and worship me." To him who had created the earth and all therein, the offer must have seemed ludicrous; but it was personal aggrandizement that the evil one sought and perhaps on a truly logical basis, for "in its present state, all this world '[had been] delivered' unto him, and he exercised the power of giving it to whom he would."[15]

In this temptation the devil sought to entice the Savior to be the earthly king that the chosen people had yearned for in their Messianic expectations (chapter 2). If he had succumbed, he might have been a satanic messiah over a temporary empire, but the Lord of lords and King of kings had to be about his Father's business, so Satan's greatest temptation became "to Christ his coarsest temptation."[16] "Get thee hence, Satan," the Lord responded, "for it is written, Thou shalt worship the Lord thy God, and him only shalt thou serve."

That the Lord had the capacity and the ability to sin (had he willed to do so) is beyond question, for otherwise he would have been denied his free agency. He had undoubtedly been tried from his youth, but he had triumphed in all things and had consistently resisted temptation.[17]

Jesus had met the dark prince of this world and had defeated him, and although he would yet be tempted again (for evil cannot be overcome in a single encounter)[18] the devil departed from him "for a season." Through his response to these temptations the Lord showed the way to the kingdom of God. Only in absolute obedience and submission to the will of the Father can victory be assured.

Jesus himself must have related these temptations to the Apostles so that they might learn that he, too, had been tempted to rebel against God's will, but he had resisted temptation because of his commitment to fulfill all righteousness.

The Transfiguration

Matthew 17:1-8

1. And after six days Jesus taketh Peter, James, and John his brother, and bringeth them up into an high mountain apart,

2. And was transfigured before them: and his face did shine as the sun, and his raiment was white as the light.

3. And, behold, there ap-

peared unto them Moses and Elias talking with him.

4. Then answered Peter, and said unto Jesus, Lord, it is good for us to be here: if thou wilt, let us make here three tabernacles; one for thee, and one for Moses, and one for Elias.

5. While he yet spake, be-

hold, a bright cloud overshad-
owed them: and behold a
voice out of the cloud, which
said, This is my beloved Son,
in whom I am well pleased;
hear ye him.

6. And when the disciples
heard it, they fell on their

face, and were sore afraid.

7. And Jesus came and
touched them, and said,
Arise, and be not afraid.

8. And when they had
lifted up their eyes, they saw
no man, save Jesus only.

Cross-references

Mark 9:2–9   Luke 9:28–36
2 Peter 1:16–18

The Apostles had been with the Lord for approximately two
years at the time of his transfiguration. He had been training them
for their ministry and teaching them the doctrines of the new kingdom. He had also revealed to them evidences of his divine sonship
so that they might recognize him as the true Messiah and eliminate
their stubborn prejudices regarding the anticipated Messiah which
had been ingrained in them from their youth.

Approximately one week prior to the Transfiguration, Jesus
asked the Apostles who people thought he was. Peter responded
that some said he was John the Baptist and others that he was the
prophet Elias. Jesus then pointedly asked the Apostles who *they*
thought he was, and Peter, responding both for himself and for the
Twelve, declared that Jesus was the Christ, the very Messiah (Matthew 16:13–19).[19] Evidently the Apostles had reached the high
point of their faith by this time.

Jesus praised them for their testimony and acknowledged that
their understanding had come from heaven, that they had received
a witness from God through the Spirit. Thereupon he immediately
began to teach them concerning his impending death and why it
was necessary. But Peter protested such an ignominious end for
the Messiah. Jesus reproved Peter for his lack of understanding,
saying, "Get thee behind me, Satan" (Matthew 16:23).

The realization that Jesus would enter his kingdom by suffering
shame and death was a shock to all of the Twelve, and it contradicted their ingrained preconceptions of the Messiah. They lacked

understanding of the Lord's spiritual mission, and they became discouraged.[20] From the high point of Peter's testimony, the spirit of the Twelve seemed to wane until the Ascension, for they had continuously exhibited an unwillingness to acknowledge His impending death and they were ill prepared to share in his sufferings, or even to believe in his resurrection.[21] "The proclamation that He was the Divine Messiah had not been met by promises of the near glory of the Messianic kingdom, but by announcements of certain, public rejection and seeming terrible defeat. Such possibilities had never seriously entered into [the Apostles'] thoughts of the Messiah."[22]

Six or eight days passed after this conversation,[23] but nothing is said of what transpired during that interval. At the end of the week, the Savior sought seclusion for the Transfiguration on a high mountain,[24] taking with him his three chief Apostles — Peter, James, and John. They would have climbed for some time, maybe not to the actual summit, but at least onto the cool heights where, on a calm, summer evening, they could pray and be instructed without interruption. Jesus wanted to complete the preparations for the remainder of his ministry and crucifixion. Knowing that they would soon possess the keys of the kingdom, he took these three Apostles with him so that he might strengthen them and fortify their testimony of him and his mission.

Whether from the day's lengthy activities or from the fatigue experienced from their climb, it appears that the Apostles were tired. After finishing their nightly devotions they wrapped themselves in their abbas and lay down on the hillside to sleep.[25] How long they slept is not noted, but according to Luke it appears that they slept long enough that they did not witness the beginning of the Transfiguration, for they were suddenly awakened by a great brilliance.

The Master was transfigured before them, and there appeared two other figures with him — Moses and "Elias" (the New Testament [Greek] form of Elijah).[26] The scriptures do not indicate how Peter, James, and John knew that it was Moses and Elijah with Jesus, but perhaps in their spiritually enlightened state and because of the splendor of the Transfiguration in which they were participating the Spirit quickened their understanding. Moses and Elijah, those two great prophets from the past who had founded and

defended the Mosaic Law, had come to perform a mission that
would supersede and fulfill the old law and make way for the gospel—the new law.

The Apostles were astounded by the three transfigured beings
before them, and they listened intently as the holy men spoke of
the upcoming death of the Messiah. One reason why Jesus had
brought Peter, James, and John with him was that they might gain
further understanding of his impending death. The experience
would give them the necessary spiritual strength to bear the sight
of his future humiliation, but at the same time would allow them
to witness the glory that he would eventually possess. These three
great men would soon lead the Lord's Church, and they needed to
be strengthened and prepared for the great authority that the
Savior would bestow upon them.

Moses and Elijah had been allowed to retain their physical
bodies so that they could confer the keys of the kingdom upon
Peter, James, and John.[27] Moses conferred the keys of the gathering of Israel, and Elijah the keys of the sealing power. All other
authority that they would need was given to them by Jesus.[28] Peter
later referred to the Transfiguration in his second epistle (2 Peter
1:16–19), and John alluded to it in his Gospel (John 1:14) and in
the opening of his first epistle to the Church (1 John 1:1–2).

The splendor of the vision they witnessed and the Transfiguration of Christ before them left the Apostles awed, confused, and
bewildered.[29] The scriptures note that they were "sore afraid," but
in spite of their fear Peter stated, "Lord, it is good for us to be
here." In fact, as Moses and Elijah departed, he suggested that
three tabernacles be built to commemorate the experience. His
naive proposal may have been intended to delay the departure of
Moses and Elijah, but the magnitude of the Transfiguration was
not over, and a bright cloud now appeared over the mount and en-
shrouded the Apostles and the Lord. The voice of the Father ema-
nated from within the cloud, proclaiming Christ as His Son and
testifying to his divinity. At the conclusion of this divine testimony the cloud dissipated, and Jesus and his Apostles were left
alone on the mountainside.

Even though the Apostles had been told about the Lord's impending death and resurrection, they still seemed unable to comprehend it, and they apparently still had no clear concept of resur-

rection.[30] However, the Transfiguration would have been a time of encouragement to the Savior, and the appearance of Moses and Elijah would have undoubtedly strengthened him, just as the ministering of angels had done after his forty-day fast and his temptations.[31]

No lengthy discussion is recorded in the scriptures between the Apostles and the Savior concerning the Transfiguration. Only the Savior's admonition is recorded: that they tell no man concerning it until after his ascension.

During the Transfiguration Jesus had comforted the Apostles because they were afraid; now, when they had an opportunity to question the Lord, their questions concerned the teachings of the Jewish leadership, which indicated that Elias must "first come." The three Apostles had just seen Elias, and Jesus informed them that the Elias spoken of by the Jewish leadership was, in fact, John the Baptist, who had come in the "spirit and power" of Elias to prepare the way before the Messiah (chapter 3). Thus the conflict in their minds between their traditional Jewish teachings and those of the Savior concerning Elias and the mission of John the Baptist was resolved.

The Transfiguration was clearly a divine attestation that Jesus was the Messiah and that his coming would fulfill the Law and supersede the Prophets.[32] The experience was a witness to Peter, James, and John that the Law of Moses and the teachings of the prophets were only preparatory to the new dispensation in which the gospel of Jesus Christ would be ushered in. From the spiritual heights of the Mount of Transfiguration the Savior would now follow his mission into the valley of humiliation and death.

Part Three

The Ministry Ends

Sacred Times

Entrance into Jerusalem

Luke 19:28–44

28. And when he had thus spoken, he went before, ascending up to Jerusalem.

29. And it came to pass, when he was come nigh to Bethphage and Bethany, at the mount called the mount of Olives, he sent two of his disciples,

30. Saying, Go ye into the village over against you; in the which at your entering ye shall find a colt tied, whereon yet never man sat: loose him, and bring him hither.

31. And if any man ask you, Why do ye loose him? thus shall ye say unto him, Because the Lord hath need of him.

32. And they that were sent went their way, and found even as he had said unto them.

33. And as they were loosing the colt, the owners thereof said unto them, Why loose ye the colt?

34. And they said, The Lord hath need of him.

35. And they brought him to Jesus: and they cast their

garments upon the colt, and they set Jesus thereon.

36. And as he went, they spread their clothes in the way.

37. And when he was come nigh, even now at the descent of the mount of Olives, the whole multitude of the disciples began to rejoice and praise God with a loud voice for all the mighty works that they had seen;

38. Saying, Blessed be the King that cometh in the name of the Lord: peace in heaven, and glory in the highest.

39. And some of the Pharisees from among the multitude said unto him, Master, rebuke thy disciples.

40. And he answered and said unto them, I tell you that, if these should hold their

peace, the stones would immediately cry out.

41. And when he was come near, he beheld the city, and wept over it,

42. Saying, If thou hadst known, even thou, at least in this thy day, the things which belong unto thy peace! but now they are hid from thine eyes.

43. For the days shall come upon thee, that thine enemies shall cast a trench about thee, and compass thee round, and keep thee in on every side,

44. And shall lay thee even with the ground, and thy children within thee; and they shall not leave in thee one stone upon another; because thou knewest not the time of thy visitation.

Cross-references

Matthew 21:1–11   Mark 11:1–11
John 12:12–20

The Jerusalem of Christ's time was a splendor to behold! It had been established as Israel's seat of government by King David and raised to its early greatness by Solomon, David's son, who had made it the center of Israel's kingdom. However, if Solomon's subjects had seen the city in Christ's time they scarcely would have recognized it. Solomon had developed and expanded Jerusalem, but Herod had truly magnified it, making it a place of beauty and splendor beyond anything before seen in the East.

The city was surrounded by a protective wall, but even within the city additional walls divided the distinctively different city areas. These inner walls had been raised during various historical periods and had originally been built for either protection or segregation.[1]

Herod's Jerusalem was divided into two major areas—the lower city and the upper city. The lower city formed the business quarter and was comprised of markets, bazaars, streets of trades, and guilds.[2] The upper city contained the palaces. The palace of the Maccabees was there, and adjacent to it was the Xystos—a large enclosure surrounded with colonnades to provide a place for popular assemblies. Also there was the palace of Annas (the patriarch of the family of high priests) and the palace of the ruling high priest, Caiaphas (his palace also housed the council chamber for the Sanhedrin and the public archives). Finally, there was the stately, magnificent palace of Herod the Great.[3]

Separated from both the business district and the palaces by its own walls and gates was the temple. Solomon built the first temple in Jerusalem, but it was comparatively small, perhaps the size of an ordinary church.[4] Herod later produced a structure of grandeur that was over forty-six years in the making.[5] It was so magnificent that the saying went abroad, "He that has not seen the Temple of Herod, has never known what beauty is."[6]

The temple was a structure of unparalleled size and splendor, its four outer walls (each approximately a thousand feet long) enclosing the sacred area.[7] It was constructed of glistening white marble, with gold overlay on many of the buildings, columns, and roofs.[8] It had been built by over ten thousand workmen, who were supervised in all phases of its construction by one thousand temple priests.[9]

During Christ's time, Jerusalem's permanent population would have ranged between 200,000 and 250,000 people (although this number would have swelled enormously during any of the Jewish festivals).[10] Christ's final entrance into Jerusalem took place during the Passover Feast, and it was at a Passover Feast that Cestus took a census of Jerusalem in order to inform Nero of the city's power. To establish this census, Cestus required the priests to number the multitudes attending the Passover Feast: they did this by counting the sacrifices offered in the temple during the Passover. They counted 256,500 sacrificial sheep, and estimated that 10 or 11 people would celebrate each sacrifice (it was not lawful for anyone to eat the feast singly, and some companies were known to have included as many as 20 people). The priests reported to Cestus that 2,700,200 Jews had come to the feast pure and holy. Because the "unclean" and the foreigners could not offer sacrifice, the estimated figure was probably below the actual total.[11]

From such an enormous congregation as this Jesus had drawn a company of five thousand men (plus women and children) into the wilderness to feed and teach.[12] One can easily understand, then, how quickly a large multitude would have gathered when Jesus made his final entrance into the city.

Jesus had declared his Messiahship many times throughout his ministry by means of miracles, parables, and sermons,[13] but he had never publicly established his claim in Jerusalem. In fact, on his previous visit to that city (during the Feast of Tabernacles), Jesus had traveled "as it were in secret" (John 7:10)—even though his family and some of his disciples had urged him to go there and openly proclaim his Messiahship to the rulers (John 7:2–5).[14]

The Lord knew that the culmination of his ministry was drawing near, and he wanted to conceal his identity no longer. The time had come for him to go into Jerusalem and give the leadership, the residents, and the celebrants the chance to openly accept or reject him.[15] He entered the Holy City as the King of kings—not as Israel's political king but as the universal Prince of Peace.

The Gospel writers place Christ's disciples in varying locations for the entrance, depending upon each writer's viewpoint.[16] For instance, Matthew and Mark do not record the events of the entrance in chronological order,[17] and from John's record it would appear that he was one of the two disciples sent by Jesus to retrieve the colt, for he records Christ's entrance from the perspective of the group which went forth from Jerusalem to meet the Savior as he approached the city. Luke and the other Synoptics record the event from the perspective of the group traveling with the Savior from Bethany.

Bethany was approximately two miles from Jerusalem on the eastern slope of Olivet.[18] There were three roads leading from Bethany to Jerusalem, and although we do not know which route the Savior took, he probably traveled the main trade road from Jericho because it would more easily accommodate the large number of disciples that were with him.[19]

A short time before this, the Lord had publicly raised Lazarus from the dead in Bethany, a spectacle so astonishing that the chief priests and Pharisees had gathered in a special council to decide what should be done with Jesus. Their conclusion was that if they did nothing, "all men [would] believe on him" (John 11:48), so after deliberation, they decided that they must put him to death. Jesus then left Bethany and went into the country of Ephraim to avoid these ill-intentioned rulers until the time of the Passover.

As the Passover approached, the excitement concerning the Lord again increased as the people anticipated his return to Jerusalem. They "sought for Jesus" and questioned whether he would come to the feast (John 11:56). Six days before the Passover, Jesus returned to Bethany and went to the home of Mary, Martha, and Lazarus (John 12:1-2).[20] News of his arrival spread throughout Jerusalem, and many came to see him (John 12:9).

On the day of his entrance (presumably at about midday or early afternoon),[21] the Lord left Bethany for Jerusalem, accompanied by many of his friends and disciples. Other disciples probably joined him along the way, and undoubtedly some rushed ahead to spread the word of his coming. The Lord's entourage would also have included those who had come to see Lazarus, as well as the curious festival celebrants who had been lodged outside the city and were now eager to take part in the day's celebration.[22]

As the group traveled they approached Bethphage, apparently a suburb of Jerusalem.[23] At this point the Lord dispatched two disciples (generally thought to have been Peter and John)[24] to procure a colt for him to ride upon as he entered Jerusalem. They were instructed to go into the village "over against you" (presumably Bethphage) to find the colt. If they were questioned by the colt's owner as to why they were taking it, they were to say that "the Lord hath need of him," and all would be well. The two Apostles did as they were instructed and soon returned leading the unbroken colt by the bridle. They were accompanied by disciples and curiosity seekers and followed by more.[25]

What the Lord did during the time it took to get the colt is not mentioned, but John's narration bears witness that many came from Jerusalem to meet the Savior. It is evident that word of his approach had reached the city and had been spread throughout the temple area,[26] because many people cut palm branches and went forth to meet him shouting praises to the "King of Israel."

It should be noted that this crowd also included some of the jealous Pharisees and other antagonists of the Lord who had watched his every move and were now bent on his destruction (Luke 19:39; John 12:19). Perhaps the group also included the lame whom he had cured, the dumb that now sang his praises, and the blind to whom he had given sight — all crowding forward that they might gaze upon their benefactor.[27] Doubtless, both groups were made up primarily of disciples and curious pilgrims who had come to the Passover festival, for "the overwhelming majority of the citizens of Jerusalem were bitterly and determinately hostile to Christ."[28]

The Lord's entourage and the celebrating multitude from Jerusalem eventually merged. Jesus was placed upon the donkey's colt, and his triumphant procession into the holy city began.

The chosen people had been conditioned to expect this public Messianic occurrence,[29] and Jesus had deliberately chosen the unridden[30] colt of a donkey as his mount for it represented his kingship over the chosen people (Zechariah 9:9).[31] Historically, Abraham had ridden a lowly donkey when he went to the holy mountain to sacrifice Isaac (Genesis 22:1–14); Moses, a chosen prophet of God, had led his wife into Egypt on such an animal (Exodus 4:20); King Ahasuerus had honored Mordecai by bringing him triumphantly into Shushan on his own horse (Esther 6:8, 11); and King David had declared Solomon his successor by placing him on his own mule to ride through Jerusalem (1 Kings 1:33). Because of historical significance and prophetic expectation, every believing Jew would have anticipated the Messiah's procession,[32] and "no act could [have been] more perfectly in keeping with the conception of a king of Israel, and no words could [have expressed] more plainly that that King proclaimed Himself the Messiah."[33] The joy of the multitude spontaneously erupted and the people cried, "Hosanna to the Son of David," and "Blessed be the King that cometh in the name of the Lord."

This salutation did not mean that all in the multitude knew that Jesus was the Messiah — their cries were partly based upon chants that the multitudes always recited on solemn festival days (Psalm 118:25–28). Further, this was the traditional greeting used by the residents of Jerusalem to welcome festive pilgrims.[34] But on this day the acclamations were accepted by Christ as the fulfillment of prophecy because they honored him as their King and their Messiah. As the people rejoiced over the Savior's ride into the city, they not only shouted praises and acclamations but also removed some of their garments and cut down palm branches and other foliage to lay along his path, making a carpet for the passing King.[35] The Pharisees' reaction was predictable — they instantly requested that the Savior quiet the crowd. But Jesus explained to the Pharisees that on this day if the crowd were quieted, the very stones would cry out proclaiming him King.

As the multitude descended from the Mount of Olives, with the city of Jerusalem in full view, Jesus paused, wept, and sadly uttered prophesies concerning the city and its residents. Generally speaking, the rulers and the inhabitants of Jerusalem had rejected the Savior and his claim to the Messiahship. Even now they objected to him, and that objection would shortly lead to his crucifixion. This, in turn, would lead to the destruction of Jerusalem and the beautiful temple that lay before them, and the Lord prophesied that the enemies of the Jews would lay seige to the city on "every side." Many would die, and the stones of the city walls that had offered them such protection and security would be leveled until all was destroyed — not one stone would be left upon another. Although no one understood his prophecy at the time, less than forty short years later it was fulfilled.

Those in the multitude and even in the city who hated the Lord and sought his destruction still craved salvation. They yearned for the Messiah that Christ claimed to be, but he refused to be their political savior. In spite of this conflict, his entrance publicly established his claim to the Messiahship, not as Israel perceived the Messiah but as the Messiah had been prophetically proclaimed (Isaiah 62:11; Zechariah 9:9).[36] So great was the cry heralding the Savior as the Son of David that the Pharisees complained in disgust that if he were left alone, all the world would go after him (John 12:19).[37]

The Lord's entry into Jerusalem occurred four days before the official Passover celebration began,[38] and the joyous shouts acclaiming him king were based on the same hymn that would be sung on the day when the paschal lamb was slain in the temple for consumption on the feast day.[39] Christ had not informed his disciples or the Twelve about the significance of his entrance into Jerusalem on this particular day, and none of them seemed to

really understand what was taking place.[40] Without this understanding they undoubtedly "walked in the procession almost as in
a dream, or as dazzled by a brilliant light all around—as if im-
pelled by a necessity, and carried from event to event, which came
upon them in a succession of but partially understood surprises."[41]
Only the Savior knew that he was offering himself as the paschal
lamb for the sins of all mankind.

Even while the people shouted hosannas and acclaimed Christ
as their king, they did not fully understand what this acclamation
entailed. They enthusiastically accepted Jesus as the prophet of
Nazareth from Galilee,[42] but he had not fulfilled their expectations
as a powerful, political leader. The Pharisees and the rulers, however, understood his claim,[43] and they watched for an opportunity
to secure his destruction.

The Last Supper, Part One:
The Passover Feast

Matthew 26:17–25

17. Now the first day of
the feast of unleavened bread
the disciples came to Jesus,
saying unto him, Where wilt
thou that we prepare for thee
to eat the passover?

18. And he said, Go into
the city to such a man, and
say unto him, The Master
saith, My time is at hand; I
will keep the passover at thy
house with my disciples.

19. And the disciples did
as Jesus had appointed them;
and they made ready the
passover.

20. Now when the even

was come, he sat down with
the twelve.

21. And as they did eat,
he said, Verily I say unto
you, that one of you shall
betray me.

22. And they were exceed-
ing sorrowful, and began
every one of them to say unto
him, Lord, is it I?

23. And he answered and
said, He that dippeth his hand
with me in the dish, the same
shall betray me.

24. The Son of man goeth
as it is written of him: but
woe unto that man by whom

the Son of man is betrayed! it had been good for that man if he had not been born.

25. Then Judas, which

betrayed him, answered and said, Master, is it I? He said unto him, Thou hast said.

Cross-references

Mark 14:12–21   Luke 22:7–16, 21–38

The Lord's triumphant entry into Jerusalem produced enormous excitement throughout the holy city and among the Passover celebrants, but as the days progressed and the feast of the Passover drew nigh, Jesus did nothing to further his claim in the people's eyes. All that they had heard from him were his discourses in the temple.[44] They undoubtedly still anticipated the powerful advent of the long-awaited Messianic kingdom, but by now it was evident that Jesus was not the one they had looked for.[45] His Messianic claims at this time and throughout his ministry had not gone unnoticed, however. From the very moment Jesus entered Jerusalem, the Jewish leadership took counsel on how they might subtly take him and kill him (Matthew 26:4). Their deliberations were cautious for they knew that many looked upon Jesus as a prophet, so they determined that they would not take him on the feast day for fear of a public uproar (Matthew 26:5). In the midst of their dilemma an unknown ally appeared: Judas Iscariot sought them out, and with diabolical avarice "Satan's serf"[46] bargained with them over the price of the Messiah's betrayal. The bargain was completed, the covenant made: they would give him thirty pieces of silver, the price of a common slave, for the betrayal of the Savior of the world.

This may have been the only Passover that Jesus celebrated as the "head" of the company rather than as a guest.[47] At the first Passover after beginning his public ministry, he had not yet called the Twelve Apostles, so if he attended the celebration at Jerusalem he would not have served at the head of the table.[48] During the second Passover he was not in Jerusalem, so he did not celebrate the feast there that year (Matthew 15:21). But on this, the third and final Passover of his mission, he gathered his group around the paschal lamb, as did all of Israel in commemoration of the past, in celebration of the present, and in keen anticipation of the future.

The scriptures report that "the day of unleavened bread came when the passover offering must be killed," so the Lord sent Peter and John to prepare the Passover feast. To properly prepare for the meal they had to acquire a male lamb, one year of age and without blemish. At "about two [2:00 P.M.], the blast of horns announced that the priests and Levites in the Temple were ready, and the gates in the inner courts were opened that all might bring their lambs for examination, and might satisfy the priests as to the number intending to consume each."[49] Peter and John would have lined up with the other men inside the temple courts, the lamb draped across their shoulders. The knife used to slay the lamb would have been stuck in its wool or tied to its horn. When the time to slaughter the lambs approached, the gates of the temple would have been shut. At about 2:30 P.M., the lamb for the evening offering was killed, and about one hour later this ceremony was completed when parts of the lamb were laid upon the altar. Three blasts of the trumpets sounded and the Levites performed choral singing, signaling the time for the slaughter of the Passover lambs.[50]

The slaughter of the lambs took place between the Jews' two evenings: the first evening was defined as the interval after the sun commenced its decline, and the second evening occurred at the hour when the sun started to disappear, or about 6:00 P.M.[51] During the ceremony, the priests held large silver bowls and golden vessels of curious shape to catch the blood of the lambs as they were slaughtered by the heads of the families. The priests passed the blood-filled containers behind them to other priests until they reached the foot of the altar, where the blood was poured out. The lambs were skinned and dressed in the temple, with the tail, fat, kidneys, and liver set apart for use at the altar. The rest of the animal was wrapped in the skin and taken by the celebrants to be placed on pomegranate wood and roasted in an underground oven in preparation for the Passover meal.[52]

The feast began immediately after the sun had officially set and the stars appeared. This event was proclaimed by trumpet blasts from the temple on what was designated as the beginning of the fifteenth of Nisan.[53]

The Lord gave curious instructions to some of his disciples for preparing the room where he and the Apostles would celebrate the Passover. He told them to go into the city, where they would meet a man bearing a pitcher of water, and follow him, for he was the goodman of the house they would use. They were to tell him that the Master would celebrate the Passover with his disciples in his guestchamber, and that when they had carried out these instructions, they would know that all would be furnished—and so it was.

When evening approached and the hour of the supper arrived, the Lord took his Twelve Apostles and went to the prepared guestchamber to celebrate the ending of the old Covenant and the beginning of the new.[54] As they commenced the last meal that the Lord would eat with them in his mortal state, a contention arose among the Twelve.

Earlier in Jesus' ministry, the Apostles had contended one with another as to who would be the greatest in his heavenly realm (Mark 9:33–34). James and John had even requested (through their mother) that they be granted the first and second positions in the Lord's kingdom (Matthew 20:20–28). Due to their lack of understanding concerning the Messiah and his mission, they longed for and sought after the honors and glories of the world.[55] The Lord once again instructed them —even on this last night before his crucifixion—using as an analogy the earthly glories and kingdoms they desired. Rather than being like the gentile kings (exercising unrighteous authority over those whom they ruled), he exhorted them to serve others. Using himself as the example, he indicated that although he was the Master of the feast, he was still sitting among them as "he that serveth."

This conflict had probably arisen over the seating arrangements at the feast table. Jewish custom places the greatest or most respected man at the head of the table, graduating down to the least important man at the foot of the table.[56] The Lord rebuked his disciples for their contention, but he would not have this evening spoiled either by their argument or by his rebuke; therefore, he continued his instructions on a positive note, acknowledging that they had indeed remained with him during his temptations and trials and promising them a place in his Father's kingdom, where they would "sit on thrones judging the twelve tribes of Israel."

The Passover table was undoubtedly set low to the ground, suspended on very short legs or braces, or perhaps it was hanging from the ceiling, suspended above the ground to preserve it from any possible Levitical defilement.[57] The table was oblong, with cushions on the floor for seating surrounding it on three sides while leaving an open end extending beyond the cushions for serving purposes. The guests reclined on the cushions rather than sitting on them, "lying on the left side and leaning on the left hand, the feet stretching back towards the ground, and each guest occupying a separate divan or pillow."[58] While differences are recorded as to the placement, description, and seating customs of the Passover table,[59] the table would probably have looked like the accompanying diagram.

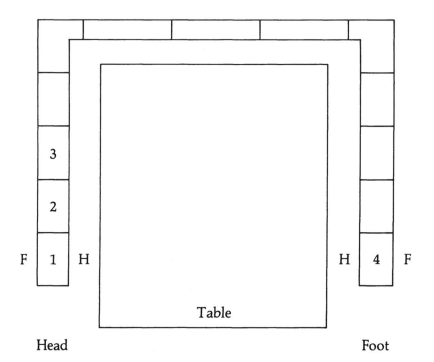

Head   Foot

Jesus, as the host of the feast, probably occupied the traditional center place of the first three cushions. This would have been the second pillow or cushion from the end, indicated by the number 2 on the diagram. As he reclined, supporting his head with his left hand, his head would have been at "H," close to the table, his feet extending beyond the cushion in the direction of "F," away from the table. Each person around the table was in a similar position.

The chief place (reserved for the chief guest of the feast) is indicated by the number 3 in the diagram, and it appears that Judas claimed that place.[60] The seat identified as number 1 in the diagram would have been occupied by John the Beloved. This would explain why, when Christ whispered to John the sign by which the traitor could be recognized, none of the other disciples heard it. In addition, if Judas occupied seat number 3 at the table, it would have been perfectly normal, in fact required, for Christ to hand him the first sop. Therefore, the other disciples would have paid no special attention when Christ handed the sop to Judas. This seating arrangement would also explain why no one seemed to hear when Judas asked the question, "Is it I?" perhaps to see if the Savior knew of his treachery. When he received an affirmative answer from the Lord, no one at the table seemed to know or understand what had passed between them.[61]

While this seating arrangement is speculative, it would also explain how easily other circumstances described in the scriptures could take place. If John was on cushion number 1, he would also have been resting on his left arm, and while leaning backward could have rested his head on the bosom of the Lord (John 13:23). While he was in this position, he asked the Lord who the traitor was.

Finally, this seating arrangement would suggest the location of one additional member of the Twelve. Peter probably occupied the seat designated by the number 4, across the table from John. Matthew 26:21 records the Lord's prophecy that one of the Apostles would betray him. Peter beckoned to John and asked him to inquire of the Lord who the traitor would be. This could have been done easily with Peter sitting immediately across the table from John. Further, it would have been the logical place for Peter to sit after the contention among the disciples concerning who should be the greatest in the Lord's kingdom. Peter, in his normal fashion and in an attempt to debase himself after the Lord's rebuke, would have naturally taken the last place at the table. The rest of the Twelve would have been seated around the table at their convenience.[62]

The Passover meal would have consisted of at least three courses: first, the Passover lamb, representing God's "passing over" the houses of the children of Israel that had been sprinkled with lamb's blood, thus sparing their firstborn; second, unleavened bread, which represented the haste with which the children of Israel had left Egypt; and third, bitter herbs, which represented the bitter lives led while the children of Israel were in bondage.[63]

As the formal Passover ceremony commenced, the Lord blessed the first cup of wine (as was the custom of the feast). He then revealed to the Apostles that this would be the last time he would eat with them until they had entered his heavenly kingdom. After blessing the cup of wine, he passed it among the Twelve so that each might drink. Jesus then arose from the table, removed his dinner garment, girded himself with a towel, and proceeded to wash the Apostles' feet.

The Last Supper, Part Two: The Washing of the Feet

John 13:1–10

1. Now before the feast of the passover, when Jesus knew that his hour was come that he should depart out of this world unto the Father, having loved his own which were in the world, he loved them unto the end.

2. And supper being ended, the devil having now put into the heart of Judas Iscariot, Simon's son, to betray him;

3. Jesus knowing that the Father had given all things into his hands, and that he was come from God, and went to God;

4. He riseth from supper, and laid aside his garments; and took a towel, and girded himself.

5. After that he poureth water into a bason, and began to wash the disciples' feet, and to wipe them with the

towel wherewith he was girded.

6. Then cometh he to Simon Peter: and Peter saith unto him, Lord, dost thou wash my feet?

7. Jesus answered and said unto him, What I do thou knowest not now; but thou shalt know hereafter.

8. Peter saith unto him, Thou shalt never wash my feet. Jesus answered him, If I wash thee not, thou hast no part with me.

9. Simon Peter saith unto him, Lord, not my feet only, but also my hands and my head.

10. Jesus saith to him, He that is washed needeth not save to wash his feet, but is clean every whit: and ye are clean, but not all.

Of the four Gospel writers, only John records the washing of the feet. The Lord likely celebrated the Passover in the traditional manner, for it was indeed the last supper of the old Covenant which Jehovah (the God of the Old Testament, incarnate in Jesus Christ) had made with the children of Israel as they left Egypt. As the old Covenant was passing away, the ordinances of the new covenant were being instituted, and the first of these ordinances was the washing of feet.[64] Jesus introduced it during the Passover supper at the time of the first symbolic hand-washing (which was a part of the ritual from the old Covenant). "Now this was the custom of the Jews under their law; wherefore, Jesus did this that the law might be fulfilled" (JST, John 13:10).

The ceremonial hand-washing was performed twice during the paschal supper, first only by the head of the company. He alone stood while the others reclined at the dinner table, thereby ritualistically distinguishing himself from all others at the supper.[65] During the second hand-washing all members of the company stood and participated, which would have made the foot-washing unnecessarily cumbersome. Therefore, while we do not know exactly when the washing of feet took place, it would have most easily been performed at the time of the first hand-washing while the Twelve were still reclining on their cushions. Thus, the Lord arose from the table after the first cup of wine had passed the lips of all present and, "during supper," removed his outer dinner garment and girded himself with a towel.[66]

Throughout his ministry the ceremonial washings as the Jews performed them had meant nothing to the Lord. Indeed, he had been criticized for not complying with them (Matthew 15:1–14; Mark 7:1–23). Jesus considered the Jews' ceremonies as nothing more than outward observances, availing nothing to those who were not inwardly clean and unnecessary to those whose hearts and lives had already been purified. He perhaps performed them now to mark the ceremonial end of the old Law.

Christ probably began by pouring water into a large copper bowl or basin that was always provided by the householder at such a meal.[67] He washed his hands in accordance with the Law and moved first to Peter, coming to him "not after the others, but after the place where the basin and water for the purification had stood."[68] It was only natural that the Lord should begin with Peter for not only was he the chief Apostle but also was probably occupying the end position at the table opposite from where the Lord had been reclining (as previously described). Further, Peter's objection to the Lord's washing his feet would hold more meaning if he were first to receive the service.

Peter's reaction was typical of his personality. He behaved similarly when he was called to follow the Savior after the miracle of the first draught of fish.[69] After his call he had fallen down at Jesus' feet and said, "Depart from me; for I am a sinful man, O Lord" (Luke 5:8). Much later in Christ's ministry, when Jesus informed the Apostles that he would die at Jerusalem, Peter again began to rebuke him, saying, "Be it far from thee, Lord: this shall not be unto thee" (Matthew 16:22). It was therefore natural that Peter object to his feet being washed by the Savior, for he considered it to be a slave's task and the lowest act of personal service.[70] The Lord's response to Peter's statement indicates that Peter did not understand the meaning of the ordinance, and in his ignorance he stubbornly maintained, "Thou shalt never wash my feet."

The Lord did not remonstrate with Peter as he had when Peter had rebuked him for forecasting His future death, but he indicated to his chief Apostle that if he did not wash his feet, Peter could have no part with him. Peter's great character and strong love for the Lord was again manifest when he immediately cried, "Lord, not my feet only, but also my hands and my head." But that was unnecessary, and the Lord indicated that washing the feet was all that was required.

This brief discussion between the Lord and Peter revealed the first reason for instituting the washing of the feet. The ordinance was necessary so that *the Apostles might have "a part" with Jesus.* To be a part with him and share his great work of salvation upon the earth, they must willingly submit to him, the Master of all. The ordinance carried with it a deep symbolic meaning regarding the service required of those who would minister in his kingdom. The Lord acknowledged that the Apostles had called him Master and he accepted that title, but he emphasized that as he had washed their feet, so they too should wash one another's feet. His example was one of service: as he had served, so they should serve. The servant was not greater than the Lord, nor was the one sent greater than the Master who sent him.

The second reason for the ordinance concerned *humility, pride, and selfish ambition.* By accepting the Lord's call the Apostles had taken up the cross and entered into his ministry, which meant that they would work as he worked, serve as he had served, and love as he had loved. The washing of feet had been more than a service for personal comfort and more than just an object lesson in humility.[71] The Apostles were being told that the ordinance symbolized both their desire to emulate the Savior and their willingness to rid themselves of pride and selfish ambition.[72]

Finally, the third reason for the washing of feet was expressed in the Lord's comment that by this ordinance the Apostles became "clean every whit." To this extent, the washing of feet was related to the washing of hands. If the Apostles were not inwardly clean prior to the washing, they would not be clean after it. The ordinance would have no meaning to those who had not properly and spiritually prepared for it, but those who were clean both in heart and spirit would be *cleansed from the blood and sins of a wicked generation.* (D&C 88:74–75, 137–41.)[73] However, not all were clean among the Twelve and the Lord emphasized that, for Judas had also participated in the ordinance. The ordinance of the washing of feet is an eternal ordinance with eternal import.[74] In the latter days it was restored with the same significance as when instituted by the Savior at his last supper (D&C 88:137–41).[75]

When he had finished washing the Apostles' feet, the Lord set aside the towel and the washing bowl, put on his dinner garment, and returned to the table to continue the paschal meal. He resumed his discussion with the Apostles by prophesying that one of the Twelve would yet betray him, a statement that deeply saddened the disciples. They hesitantly began questioning, "Is it I?" "Is it I?" Peter asked John to inquire of the Lord concerning the betrayer's identity, and the Lord stated that it would be he to whom the first sop was given. It may seem odd that the disciples did not therefore recognize the betrayer when the sop was handed to Judas, but it need only be remembered that Judas, seated as the chief guest of the feast, was the first to receive the sop in any instance, and that after this, *each* of those at the table would in turn receive a sop. The "sop" was a portion of a thin flexible bread-cake dipped in the common dish,[76] and Jesus would have given one to each paschal participant in accord with the established ritual.

As Jesus prepared the first sop, Judas, perhaps fearing that he might be discovered by the others, asked, "Is it I?" While the others had asked the question in anguish of heart, Judas asked with subtlety so that he might not betray himself. However, by his uttering this question his mask of treachery was torn away, and the Lord responded, "That thou doest, do quickly."

Even now the others did not fully understand, for they undoubtedly did not hear what had taken place and they were confused. But the devil had entered into Judas and he hastened to leave the feast, while the others thought that he had gone on some errand on instruction from the Lord.[77]

After the traitor left, the atmosphere seemed to clear and the Lord appeared to be more relaxed and at ease. He spoke as though his mission was fulfilled, and he declared that the Son of Man was glorified and the Father was glorified in him. He continued to instruct the disciples, informing them that he would be with them only a short time longer: after he was gone they would seek after him, but they could not go where he was going.

Then Jesus, again declared the new commandment, that they should love one another as he had loved them and that by this all men would know that they were his disciples. Peter again showed his lack of understanding and preparedness for the approaching events[78] when he asked the Lord where He would go. The Lord responded that Peter could not go with him immediately, but that he would follow later. Again Peter protested that he would lay down his life for the Lord, whereupon the Lord cautioned him, "Simon, Simon, behold, Satan hath desired to have you."

The Lord then strengthened Peter by declaring that he had prayed that Peter's faith would not fail. He then concluded by stating that when Peter was finally converted, he should strengthen his brethren. But Peter would not relent. He again protested, stating that he was ready to go with the Lord both to prison and to death. Finally the Lord prophesied to Peter that the "cock shall not crow this day, before that thou shalt thrice deny that thou knowest me."[79]

The paschal meal continued, and undoubtedly during its normal course Jesus instituted the second ordinance of the new covenant — the sacrament.

The Last Supper, Part Three: The Sacrament

Matthew 26:26-29

26. And as they were eating, Jesus took bread, and blessed it, and brake it, and gave it to the disciples, and said, Take, eat; this is my body.

27. And he took the cup, and gave thanks, and gave it to them, saying, Drink ye all of it;

28. For this is my blood of the new testament, which is shed for many for the remission of sins.

29. But I say unto you, I will not drink henceforth of this fruit of the vine, until that day when I drink it new with you in my Father's kingdom.

Cross-references

Mark 14:22-25   Luke 22:17-20
JST, Matthew 26:22-25   3 Nephi 9:17, 19-20; 18:5-11; 20:8
Moroni 4, 5   D&C 20:75-79; 27:2-4

Only the Synoptics record the institution of the sacrament. Although there are some discrepancies between the Synoptic writings, they are insignificant. More important, they each attest to the significance of the sacrament and its institution as the emblem of the new covenant.

The Passover celebration commemorated the blessings Jehovah gave to the children of Israel as they escaped from Egyptian bondage. Included in the celebration was the slaying of the paschal lamb, an act which looked forward to the anticipated Messiah. This represented part of the ancient sacrifice practiced by Adam in anticipation of the future Atonement and sacrifice of the Son of God (Moses 5:5–8).[80]

From the Exodus forward, the children of Israel had celebrated the Passover in the similitude of Christ's sacrifice. "All of the sacrificial similitudes of all ages combined to bear testimony of the infinite and eternal atoning sacrifice—the sacrifice of the Lamb of God who taketh away the sins of the world."[81]

Now Christ's eternal sacrifice was about to take place, and the paschal lambs that had been slain in the temple symbolically testified for the last time of that great and eternal sacrifice that would shortly come to pass. When Christ gave his life for mankind, animal sacrifice authorized by the Lord, as it was practiced from Adam to the time of Christ, ceased. At the Last Supper, the Lord instituted a new ordinance to replace it. The new ordinance was called the sacrament.

The Passover meal offered the perfect situation for instituting the sacrament. The similitude of the Passover celebration and that of the sacrament was the same. Whereas the ceremonial sacrifice of animals looked forward to the great eternal sacrifice, the shedding of blood and the atonement of Christ for all mankind, the sacrament looked to the past in remembrance of that glorious event. Both ordinances focus on that moment in time when the Son of God fulfilled his earthly mission and provided through the Atonement, the Crucifixion, and the Resurrection (1) salvation for all mankind and (2) exaltation for those who would obey his words. The blood of the Passover lamb redeemed God's chosen people from the angel of death as it passed over Egypt; so, too, the blood of the Son of God will ransom all mankind from the angel of death (sin) and thus open the way for entering God's kingdom.

After Christ washed the Apostle's feet, the supper continued. The company no doubt ate bitter herbs in remembrance of the children of Israel's sojourn in Egypt. Whether the Lord participated in every portion of the ceremonial observance is unknown, but it is unlikely that he did so, for the Jewish leaders had changed and expanded much of the ceremony over the passing centuries.[82] However, they certainly ate all the unleavened bread and the lamb, for the feast required it. At this point, the ceremony called for the blessing and drinking of the third cup of wine, and in all probability it was now that the Lord instituted the ordinance of the sacrament.[83]

Just as with the washing of feet, the ceremony of the Passover feast provided the Lord with the opportunity of instituting a new ordinance without unduly disrupting the supper itself. He took bread, "blessed it, and brake it, and gave it to the disciples," with the instructions that they should eat, for, he said, "This is my body." Similarly, he took the cup, "gave thanks, and gave it to them," instructing them to drink, for, he said, "This is my blood of the New Testament, which is shed for many for the remission of sins." The scriptures note that the Lord blessed both the bread and the wine, but the specific words of the blessings are not recorded. Although the Passover celebration contained certain ritual blessings for the bread and the wine,[84] the Lord probably would not have used them.[85] Although the New Testament does not record specific instructions regarding the sacrament, the Book of Mormon does. It explains that after Christ's resurrection, he visited the Nephites and instituted the sacrament (3 Nephi 18:3–11). In this connection, no doubt the Lord gave the same instructions to the Apostles of the ancient Church as he did to the Nephites and to the latter-day prophet of the Restoration.[86] These include the sacrament prayers, the similitudes of the bread to Christ's body, the wine to his blood; and the teaching that by worthily partaking of the sacrament we come into fellowship with him and spiritually feed on the remembrance of his mission. (See 3 Nephi 18:3–11; Moroni 4, 5; D&C 20:75–79.)

The Lord used wine for the sacrament both at the Last Supper and on the Western Hemisphere. However, in the Restoration the Lord revealed that water could be substituted for wine (D&C 27:2–4), as we do today.

We take the sacrament for the following purposes:

(1) To remember the body and blood of Christ. The ordinance looks back on the Atonement, the Crucifixion, and the Resurrection. Like sacrifice, the Passover celebration had looked forward to those same events. Through our remembrance we acknowledge that Jesus is the resurrection and the life, and no one can be saved but by him (John 14:6).

(2) To take upon us the name of Christ. We covenant with and witness before our Father in Heaven that we will take upon us the name of Christ. By doing this we accept Christ's teachings and place them in our lives as guiding principles. Earlier in his ministry, Jesus alluded to this when he delivered a discourse at Capernaum on "the bread of life."[87] In that discourse he used the common metaphors of food and drink[88] to teach the Jews that they must "eat of his flesh" and "drink of his blood" to become part of him. The literal-minded Jews questioned how anyone could eat of his flesh and drink of his blood, but the Lord was using the example metaphorically, not literally. He meant that they must make his teachings and their belief in him part of them and that they should exemplify that belief in everything they did, just as bread and wine were assimilated into their body tissues and literally became an abiding part of the body. When we partake the sacrament worthily we accept Christ as our Lord and King, and we evidence this by living his commandments and acknowledging him as the literal Son of God, our personal Savior.

(3) To always remember him. We should direct our constant attention to the Savior's atonement. In celebrating the final feast of the Passover, the Lord fulfilled the old law and initiated the new. "Sacrifice stopped and sacrament started."[89] Sacrifice and the Passover pointed the ancients *toward* the coming atonement, the sacrament replaced these venerable ordinances and pointed the attention of his Saints (after his death) *back* to the great atoning sacrifice which he had wrought.[90]

(4) To keep the Lord's commandments. We specifically covenant to keep the Lord's commandments when we partake of the sacrament. The Lord put it simply: "If ye love me, keep my commandments" (John 14:15). To keep his commandments is to "live by every word that proceedeth forth from the mouth of God" (D&C 84:44).

(5) To receive God's blessings. Providing we have partaken of the sacrament worthily and continue to live righteously, God has promised us that he will grant us his Spirit to be with us so that "in due course [all] shall inherit eternal life."[91]

The Church grew rapidly after Christ's resurrection, and the Apostles undoubtedly instructed the new converts in proper sacrament observance. The Savior had instituted a simple rite; however, various incorrect doctrines developed concerning the sacrament until its restoration in modern times. Perhaps these changes were due to theological zeal or heated fancy, but in any event they would have startled and shocked the original Saints.

Evidence of this problem was apparent early in the Church. The Saints at Corinth had made a mockery of the sacrament by reducing it to a gluttonous feast replete with drunkenness. Paul, in correcting this wrongdoing, declared harshly, "For there must be also heresies among you. . . . When ye came together therefore into one place, this is not to eat the Lord's supper. For in eating every one taketh before other his own supper: and one is hungry, and another is drunken. What? have ye not houses to eat and to drink in? or despise ye the church of God, and shame them that have not? What shall I say to you? shall I praise you in this? I praise you not." (1 Corinthians 11:19–22.)

Paul warned the Saints not to make a mockery of this ordinance nor participate in it unworthily, concluding that if a man did so, he would eat and drink "damnation to himself. . . . For this cause many are weak and sickly among you, and many sleep [die]." (1 Corinthians 11:27–30.)

The sacrament is a simple ordinance but is of singular importance in the lives of worthy Saints. If we partake of it unworthily we jeopardize our salvation, but if we partake worthily we open the door to eternal life by accepting Christ and his teachings into our lives.

When the Savior had finished administering the sacrament to the Apostles, he continued his teachings to strengthen their faith. The fateful advent of his arrest and trial would soon scatter them abroad, so he reminded them of the success of their first mission. They had gone without purse or scrip and yet lacked nothing, and the Apostles acknowledged this. But now the Lord told them to be prepared, to *take* purse and scrip, for now they would be subject to the harsh circumstances of the world. The sword, he said as an example, would better describe their future proselytizing problems: if they did not have a sword they should sell their garments and buy one. It was another metaphor used to describe the difficult times they would face as they taught all nations. He knew that he and his followers would be "reckoned among the transgressors" in the world's eyes. The Apostles again failed to grasp the Lord's meaning and declared they had but two swords in their possession. Without continuing his explanation Jesus closed the conversation by simply stating, "It is enough" (Luke 22:38).

The Passover supper was finished—the old Covenant had passed away.

In the Valley of the Shadow of Death

6

The Atonement

Matthew 26:31–45

31. Then saith Jesus unto them, All ye shall be offended because of me this night: for it is written, I will smite the shepherd, and the sheep of the flock shall be scattered abroad.

32. But after I am risen again, I will go before you into Galilee.

33. Peter answered and said unto him, Though all men shall be offended because of thee, yet will I never be offended.

34. Jesus said unto him, Verily I say unto thee, That this night, before the cock crow, thou shalt deny me thrice.

35. Peter said unto him, Though I should die with thee, yet will I not deny thee. Likewise also said all the disciples.

36. Then cometh Jesus with them unto a place called Gethsemane, and saith unto the disciples, Sit ye here, while I go and pray yonder.

37. And he took with him Peter and the two sons of Zebedee, and began to be sorrowful and very heavy.

38. Then saith he unto them, My soul is exceeding sorrowful, even unto death: tarry ye here, and watch with me.

39. And he went a little further, and fell on his face, and prayed, saying, O my Father, if it be possible, let this cup pass from me: nevertheless not as I will, but as thou wilt.

40. And he cometh unto the disciples, and findeth them asleep, and saith unto Peter, What, could ye not watch with me one hour?

41. Watch and pray, that ye enter not into temptation: the spirit indeed is willing, but the flesh is weak.

42. He went away again the second time, and prayed, saying, O my Father, if this cup may not pass away from me, except I drink it, thy will be done.

43. And he came and found them asleep again: for their eyes were heavy.

44. And he left them, and went away again, and prayed the third time, saying the same words.

45. Then cometh he to his disciples, and saith unto them, Sleep on now, and take your rest: behold, the hour is at hand, and the Son of man is betrayed into the hands of sinners.

Cross-references

Mark 14:27–41   Luke 22:40–46
JST, Mark 14:36

At the conclusion of the Passover supper, Jesus and the eleven Apostles prepared to leave Jerusalem to go to the Mount of Olives. The temple gates on this festive night were thrown open at midnight,[1] and the streets were not deserted. As they passed the houses, bright lamps may have illuminated the night, indicating that the celebration of the paschal lamb was still taking place.

The group passed out of the city through the gate north of the temple and descended into the Valley of Kidron, then crossed over to the other side of the valley and entered the garden known as Gethsemane. *Gethsemane* means "oil press,"[2] and was derived from the fact that there was an olive grove growing there.[3] As they walked toward the garden the Lord stated that all of them would be "offended . . . this night" because of him and that the "sheep of the flock" would be scattered abroad. Matthew reports that Peter protested, but the Lord prophesied that Peter would deny knowing him "thrice" before the cock crowed. Again he protested, stating that he would die before denying the Savior, as did all the disciples.

Leaving eight of the Apostles at Gethsemane's entrance, the Lord took Peter, James, and John with him into the garden. As they progressed deeper into the garden, Jesus became heavy with sorrow. Then the Lord asked these three Apostles to tarry and watch with him. He went on ahead, "fell on his face," and prayed to his Father in Heaven. John records some of this personal conversation between the Son and the Father (John 17),[4] and the Synoptics record the agony of the occasion when even the Savior of the world prayed, "If it be possible, let this cup pass from me: nevertheless not as I will, but as thou wilt."

As the Lord continued in prayer, he took upon himself the burden of the fall of Adam and all the subsequent sins of mankind: in so doing he prepared the way by which all again could return into the Father's presence. Meantime, the Apostles became weary and fell asleep (just as they had done on the Mount of Transfiguration —Luke 9:32). About an hour later the Lord returned to them. He roused them from their slumber and admonished Peter, "Could ye not watch with me one hour?" Again he earnestly requested them to watch and pray lest they enter into temptation, then he returned to his prayers. The Apostles apparently watched for a time, heeding the caution from the Lord, for a limited amount of the Lord's second prayer is recorded. Matthew records that the Lord, fully recognizing his mission, commented that the cup *could not* pass from him — the Father's will would be done.

Luke's gospel records the Lord's agony in detail. He writes that an angel appeared to Jesus to strengthen him, causing him to pray even more earnestly. The pain of suffering for the sins of mankind was so great that "his sweat was as great drops of blood falling down to the ground." The prayers continued, but again the Apostles became "heavy" and fell asleep. When the Lord returned and found them asleep once more, he again roused them. He immediately returned to pray for the third time, "saying the same words." When he had completed his prayers, the Lord returned and found the Apostles asleep for the third time. He did not immediately awaken them but allowed them to sleep on, for the hour was at hand when the Son of God would be betrayed into the hands of his enemies. (Perhaps at least one Apostle was awake from time to time or [apart from the possibility of later revelation] there would be no record of Jesus' prayers, but they all must have been asleep when the Lord returned to them.) It is impossible for the finite mind to understand or comprehend the unbearable physical and spiritual agony that the Son of God experienced in the Garden, but in spite of his anguish he remained faithful to his Father and to his calling.

At the commencement of his mission the Lord had contended with the devil three times at the end of his fast in the wilderness; now, as his earthly mission was ending, he overcame all that Satan had done or would ever do.[5] There is no question that the pain and suffering of the crucifixion was part of Christ's atonement, but "the triumph and grandeur of the atonement took place primarily in Gethsemane."[6]

Just how the Savior of the world took upon himself the sins of mankind to intercede for the faithful is unknown, but that this was the Messiah's ultimate purpose in his earthly ministry is attested to by all of the prophets. Jesus had come to earth to assume the total burden of man's sin and shame, to overcome the Apostasy and the Fall, and to taste of "the bitter cup which sin had poisoned."[7] Failure would have allowed Satan to succeed. Death, both physical and spiritual, separated mankind from the Father, and only through an infinite sacrifice by one such as the Son of God could the Fall be overcome and man be reunited with his Father in Heaven.

Amuluk bore testimony of the great atoning sacrifice of the Lord in these words:

> I do know that Christ shall come among the children of men, to take upon him the transgressions of his people, and that he shall atone for the sins of the world; for the Lord God hath spoken it.
>
> For it is expedient that an atonement should be made; for according to the great plan of the Eternal God there must be an atonement made, or else all mankind must unavoidably perish; yea, all are hardened; yea, all are fallen

and are lost, and must perish except it be through the atonement which it is expedient should be made.

For it is expedient that there should be a great and last sacrifice; yea, not a sacrifice of man, neither of beast, neither of any manner of fowl; for it shall not be a human sacrifice; but it must be an infinite and eternal sacrifice.

Now there is not any man that can sacrifice his own blood which will atone for the sins of another. . . .

. . . Therefore there can be nothing which is short of an infinite atonement which will suffice for the sins of the world. (Alma 34:8-12.)

Through the Atonement, the fall of Adam was overcome and victory over death secured (1 Corinthians 15:22; Romans 5:12-18). The ransom had been paid and the Lord's mastery over Satan was finally complete. Adam had introduced spiritual and temporal death into the world, but the "second Adam" (1 Corinthians 15:45-47) had provided the opportunity for eternal life.

With the Fall overcome, man was now fully responsible for his own sins. Christ's suffering made operable the law whereby each individual could lay claim to the blessings of the Atonement — that law was repentance. Without repentance God's justice applies to every sin, and man is forever banned from his presence. However, repentance and God's mercy satisfy the demands of justice, making it possible for the eternal plan of redemption to automatically apply (Alma 34:15-16; 2 Peter 3:9). Although the Atonement is difficult to comprehend, its application is not — simply stated, the Atonement made operable the law of repentance.

While the Lord prayed intensely in Gethsemane and the Apostles slept, Judas consummated his sinful plot with the chief priests. The Savior returned for the last time to his slumbering Apostles and, perhaps as he sat and watched, his ears might have caught the noise of treading footsteps and the ill-suppressed tumult of the advancing crowd. The traitor knew of the quiet garden, for he had been there often (John 18:2). Soon the red glare of torches could be seen, and Jesus awakened his sleeping brethren. As Judas, the authorities, and the rest of the crowd approached, the Lord sadly spoke his last free words to his confused Apostles, "He is at hand that doth betray me" (Matthew 26:46).

Never once did the Lord waver from the Father's will. Jesus alone could take upon himself the burden of the sins of mankind, and he alone could suffer the torture and spiritual agony of soul that caused him to "bleed from every pore." No ordinary man could have suffered so.

In March 1830 the resurrected and glorified Savior revealed the following about the agonizing atoning experience he undertook for all mankind:

> For behold, I, God, have suffered these things for all, that they might not suffer if they would repent;
> But if they would not repent they must suffer even as I;
> Which suffering caused myself, even God, the greatest of all, to tremble because of pain, and to bleed at every pore, and to suffer both body and spirit — and would that I might not drink the bitter cup, and shrink —
> Nevertheless, glory be to the Father, and I partook and finished my preparations unto the children. (D&C 19:16–19.)

The Betrayal

Matthew 26:14–16, 21–25, 46–56

14. Then one of the twelve, called Judas Iscariot, went unto the chief priests,

15. And said unto them, What will ye give me, and I will deliver him unto you? And they covenanted with him for thirty pieces of silver.

16. And from that time he sought opportunity to betray him.

21. And as they did eat [the Passover supper], he [Christ] said, Verily I say unto you, that one of you shall betray me.

22. And they were ex-ceeding sorrowful, and began every one of them to say unto him, Lord, is it I?

23. And he answered and said, He that dippeth his hand with me in the dish, the same shall betray me.

24. The Son of man goeth as it is written of him: but woe unto that man by whom the Son of man is betrayed! it had been good for that man if he had not been born.

25. Then Judas, which betrayed him, answered and said, Master, is it I? He said unto him, Thou hast said.

[At the conclusion of the Passover supper, the Lord retired to the Garden of Gethsemane on the Mount of Olives to pray. After he had finished praying he said to his Apostles]

46. Rise, let us be going: behold, he is at hand that doth betray me.

47. And while he yet spake, lo, Judas, one of the twelve, came, and with him a great multitude with swords and staves, from the chief priests and elders of the people.

48. Now he that betrayed him gave them a sign, saying, Whomsoever I shall kiss, that same is he: hold him fast.

49. And forthwith he came to Jesus, and said, Hail, master; and kissed him.

50. And Jesus said unto him, Friend, wherefore art thou come? Then came they, and laid hands on Jesus, and took him.

51. And, behold, one of them which were with Jesus stretched out his hand, and drew his sword, and struck a servant of the high priest's, and smote off his ear.

52. Then said Jesus unto him, Put up again thy sword into his place: for all they that take the sword shall perish with the sword.

53. Thinkest thou that I cannot now pray to my Father, and he shall presently give me more than twelve legions of angels?

54. But how then shall the scriptures be fulfilled, that thus it must be?

55. In that same hour said Jesus to the multitudes, Are ye come out as against a thief with swords and staves for to take me? I sat daily with you teaching in the temple, and ye laid no hold on me.

56. But all this was done, that the scriptures of the prophets might be fulfilled. Then all the disciples forsook him, and fled.

Matthew 27:3–10

3. Then Judas, which had betrayed him, when he saw that he was condemned, repented himself, and brought again the thirty pieces of silver to the chief priests and elders,

4. Saying, I have sinned

in that I have betrayed the innocent blood. And they said,
What is that to us? see thou
to that.

5. And he cast down the
pieces of silver in the temple,
and departed, and went and
hanged himself.

6. And the chief priests
took the silver pieces, and
said, It is not lawful for to
put them into the treasury,
because it is the price of
blood.

7. And they took coun-
sel, and bought with them the

potter's field, to bury
strangers in.

8. Wherefore that field
was called, The field of
blood, unto this day.

9. Then was fulfilled that
which was spoken by Jeremy
the prophet, saying, And they
took the thirty pieces of
silver, the price of him that
was valued, whom they of the
children of Israel did value;

10. And gave them for the
potter's field, as the Lord appointed me.

Cross-references

Mark 14:10–11, 18–21, 42–50   Luke 22:1–6, 21–23, 47–53
John 13:18–31; 18:1–11

The Son of the Living God was betrayed by Judas Iscariot, a
member of the Quorum of the Twelve Apostles who had been
with Christ from the earliest times of his ministry[8] and who had
participated in all of the experiences the Twelve had had during
the Lord's mission (other than those specific times when only
Peter, James, and John had been allowed to participate).

Jesus forewarned the Apostles early in his ministry that one of
them would betray him. After the feeding of the five thousand, he
returned to Capernaum and delivered the sermon on the bread of
life.[9] This sermon was difficult for many of his followers to comprehend, so they murmured and said, "This is an hard saying; who
can hear it?" (John 6:60.) After Jesus questioned their murmuring,
"from that time many of his disciples went back, and walked no
more with him" (John 6:66). No doubt many of the disciples were
disenchanted because Jesus was not the politically powerful Messiah their Jewish traditions anticipated.

It seems that some of the Twelve may also have expressed res-
ervations, for the Lord asked them, "Will ye also go away?" (John

6:67.) Peter then stepped forth and as spokesman for the Twelve said, "Lord, to whom shall we go? thou hast the words of eternal life" (John 6:68). He confessed his belief in Christ, acknowledging that Jesus was the Son of God.

In response, the Lord told his Apostles that although he had chosen them, one of them was a devil (John 6:70). John, writing this account after the death of Jesus and with the benefit of hindsight, records, "He spake of Judas Iscariot, the son of Simon: for he it was that should betray him, being one of the Twelve" (John 6:71).

Clearly the Lord knew long before the occurrence took place that he would be betrayed. However, it is unclear whether any of the Twelve were particularly concerned about this prophecy at that time. Even though both the Savior and the ancient prophets (Zechariah 11:12) had prophesied the betrayal, it came about through seemingly normal means, in keeping with the social, political, and religious atmosphere of the day wherein Satan was allowed to deceive the chosen people and their leadership.[10]

Throughout Christ's early ministry, the rulers of the Jews followed and taunted him and constantly questioned him.[11] At times when people heard his claim to the Messiahship, they took him out and attempted to stone him (John 8:59; 10:31, 39) or to throw him from a hilltop (Luke 4:28–29). By the close of his ministry, the mindset of the leadership was such that when Mary and Martha informed the Savior of Lazarus's illness and he decided to return to Jerusalem that he might "awake him out of sleep" (John 11:11), the disciples voiced great concern, noting that "the Jews of late sought to stone thee; and goest thou thither again?" (John 11:8.) They were so concerned that Thomas boldly stepped forth and told his fellow disciples, "Let us also go, that we may die with him" (John 11:16).

Jesus returned to Jerusalem and performed the spectacular miracle of raising Lazarus from the dead,[12] which was immediately reported to the Jewish leadership. That leadership then gathered together to decide what to do with the Savior. They noted that he had performed many miracles and that if he were left alone "all men [would] believe on him" (John 11:48). Their concern was self-centered—they did not care whether Jesus was the Messiah. If Jesus was allowed to continue, they rationalized, the Romans would "come and take away both our place and nation" (John 11:48).

From "that day forth they took counsel together for to put him to death" (John 11:53); in addition, they spied on Jesus and let it be known that "if any man knew where he were, he should shew it, that they might take him" (John 11:57). Through the natural animosity which the rulers of the Jews had towards the Lord, and because he had failed their political expectations of the Messiah (besides the fact that they did not want to give up their worldly possessions and positions), they would not accept him. In their zealous concern for self-preservation and national independence, they determined that they would take the life of the very one who had come to preserve them: they only sought the most acceptable method by which they could accomplish their task.

Two days before the Feast of the Passover, the chief priests, the scribes, and the elders gathered together at the palace of Caiaphas, the high priest, to consult with one another on how they might take Jesus "by subtilty, and kill him" (Matthew 26:4). Their concern was not for Christ's guilt or innocence, or even for justice under the Jewish law, but that they might not arrest him on the feast day, "lest there be an uproar among the people" (Matthew 26:5). At this point Judas appeared on the scene. He was an ally which they could not have hoped for, for to attempt to subvert one of the Lord's own Apostles was undoubtedly a plot beyond their wildest dreams. Nonetheless, Judas Iscariot, a divinely called and ordained Apostle, "went unto the chief priests."

Judas was reportedly from the town of Kerioth, the only Judean among the Twelve Apostles. He served as treasurer for the Twelve, both receiving and disbursing their common funds.[13] John (again with the benefit of hindsight) notes that from the very beginning Judas was unprincipled and dishonest in this trust (John 12:6). His basic concern was with worldly things, as exemplified in his complaint regarding what he felt was the waste of expensive oil that Mary used to anoint Jesus' feet before his crucifixion (John 12:1-7). As he met with the chief priests prior to the Lord's arrest, his avarice was openly displayed when he furtively asked, "What will ye give me, and I will deliver him [Christ] unto you?"

Selfishness, greed, and dishonesty had turned his love for the Savior into hate and envy, and in satanic determination he avowedly "sold his soul to another master whose disciple and follower he thus became."[14]

The Sanhedrists with which Judas met were only too glad to receive him, for Judas solved their problem of how they might destroy the Savior. Although they did indeed covenant "with him for thirty pieces of silver," they "treated Judas not as an honoured associate, but as a common informer, and a contemptible traitor."[15] With the bargain struck, Zechariah's prophecy was fulfilled (Zechariah 11:12), and the temple money (which had been given for the purchase of sacrifices) would now be used to purchase the Savior — he was "bought at the legal price of a slave" (Exodus 21:32).[16]

Judas rejoined the Lord and the Twelve, participating in those events which led up to the Passover supper. He was there when the Savior commenced the Passover celebration, and he received the washing of the feet. He listened as the Savior prophesied that one among them would betray him. Unable to restrain himself as the others questioned, "Is it I?, Is it I?" he had the audacity to also exclaim, "Master, Is it I?" The Lord simply responded, "Thou hast said, that thou doest, do quickly." Judas left the supper chamber and disappeared into the night.

While Judas and the wicked Jewish leaders organized the arresting band, the Lord concluded the Passover supper and retired to the Garden of Gethsemane. After he had concluded his prayers to his Father in Heaven, he returned to Peter, James, and John, where, for the third time, he found them asleep. Not awakening them immediately, he indicated that they should rest to strengthen them against the coming events.

Exactly how much time elapsed between the Savior's return to the three sleeping Apostles and when he commanded them to arise is unknown, but when he heard the group that was coming to arrest him he awakened Peter, James, and John, commanding them, "Rise, let us be going" (Matthew 26:46). He probably took the three Apostles and returned to the Garden's entrance where he had left the remaining eight. John described the group that came to arrest Christ as a "band of men and officers from the chief priests and Pharisees, [that] cometh thither with lanterns and torches and weapons" (John 18:3). Luke described the group as a "multitude."

John points out that Judas knew the place where Jesus would

be (John 18:2), but it may have been that the arresting party had first gone to the upper room where the Last Supper had taken place and, not finding Jesus there, had proceeded on to the Garden of Gethsemane.[17] The group included some of the Jewish leadership and undoubtedly some of those who had been in the treacherous meetings between Judas and the chief priests. Perhaps others had also gathered as the group went from the temple to the garden, and certainly some of the Roman guard in Jerusalem would have been present.[18] Although the arresting group was large, it was not a multitude in the sense used to describe such situations as the feeding of the five thousand.

As the band approached with Judas at its head, Jesus "went out" to meet them. Judas hailed the Master and saluted him with a kiss (Matthew 26:50), which was the designated sign by which he would identify the Savior and betray him into the hands of the arresting party. Jesus turned to him and asked poignantly, "Judas, betrayest thou the Son of man with a kiss?" (Luke 22:48.) It appears that Jesus then walked past Judas and went towards the arresting officers, asking, "Whom seek ye?" The response was, "Jesus of Nazareth," and Jesus immediately answered, "I am he." As Jesus acknowledged who he was, the front lines of the arresting party fell back, and the action caused some of the crowd to stumble and fall. Again the Lord asked, "Whom seek ye?" and they replied the second time, "Jesus of Nazareth." The Lord answered, "I have told you that I am he: if therefore ye seek me, let these [the Apostles] go their way" (John 18:8). It was probably at this point (or just prior to the second request) that Peter drew his sword and struck off the ear of Malchus, the servant of the high priest. The Lord immediately rebuked the action and there, in the midst of his enemies, performed his last public miracle by healing the wounded ear.[19] After this the eleven Apostles forsook him and fled. Their flight was undoubtedly precipitated by their relatively untried condition,[20] but with the Lord's comments to Peter that he had legions of angels at his command but would not use them, perhaps the Apostles finally recognized that he would not call upon his supernatural powers to intervene—so they fled.

After the miracle of Malchus's ear (which apparently went unnoticed by the malicious crowd bent only on the Savior's arrest and destruction), the band laid hands on Jesus and bound him.

The Lord immediately protested his rights under the Jewish law, indicating that they had come out by night to take him. He further exclaimed, "[I] sat daily with you teaching in the temple, and ye laid no hold on me": but the hour of his enemies had come and the powers of darkness were succeeding. With the Lord safely in their custody, the crowd took him before Annas, the father-in-law of the high priest.

(The scriptures record one additional event in the arrest of the Savior. A young man had remained behind to watch the proceedings after the Apostles had scattered. The young man is unnamed but is believed to be Mark, author of the second Gospel. As the servants of the high priest noticed him they attempted to lay hold on him, and as he struggled loose from their grasp, the linen garment that he had wrapped around his body was torn from him and he fled naked into the night.)[21]

The betrayal precipitated the Savior's trial, crucifixion, and death. Christ was fulfilling all that the Father expected of him, which would serve to exemplify the teachings of his entire ministry and would culminate in his glorious resurrection. After he had risen from the tomb he would return to the glory that he had had with his Father.

The betrayal would also result in Judas Iscariot's death, but for him the rewards would be diametrically opposite. Having received the thirty pieces of silver, he "repented himself" and attempted to return the money to the chief priests and elders because he had sinned by betraying innocent blood. This was not repentance in the scriptural sense, "but a change of mind and feeling came over him."[22] Judas had left his old Master, and now his new master (Satan) had abandoned him. But the leaders had no more compassion or respect for Judas in his attempt to return the tainted silver than they had had when they covenanted with him to betray Jesus in the first place. "What is that to us?" they taunted. Judas, in utter despair over the great sin that he had committed, cast the thirty pieces of silver into the temple and went and hanged himself.[23]

The
Trials

After Jesus was arrested, he was bound (presumably by Roman soldiers) and led from the Garden of Gethsemane. The authorities had designed the Lord's capture to occur when he was relatively alone, thus creating as little disturbance as possible among the Passover celebrants.

Their objective was quite clear: proceed with the trials as rapidly as possible, find Jesus guilty, and turn him over to the Romans for execution. They could thus (1) present Jesus before the people at Jerusalem as one already accused and judged and (2) submit him to the Roman authorities in such a state that they would execute him immediately.[1]

Because the Gospels do not agree on exactly what transpired between the Savior's arrest and his crucifixion, the story must be pieced together using all four.[2]

Between the time of Christ's last supper (approximately 10:00 P.M. on Thursday) and that of his crucifixion and death (3:00 P.M. the next day) events transpired very rapidly. The trials themselves were concluded by about 9:00 A.M. Friday. The format followed in this book shows Christ being taken first to Annas (even though no record of that interview is available),[3] then on to three hearings before the Jewish leadership, who were empowered to judge. The first hearing is a private interview before Caiaphas; the second a public hearing before Caiaphas and the Sanhedrists; and the third, another hearing before Caiaphas and the Sanhedrists held early in the morning — thus providing two trials as required under Jewish law. The Lord was then taken to Pilate. Pilate sent him for an interview with Herod, but Herod soon returned him to Pilate — who then condemned and crucified him.

The Trials and the Authorities

The scriptural record that follows is an amalgamation of the four Gospels, followed by additional references.

John 18:12. Then the band and the captain and officers of the Jews took Jesus, and bound him,

John 18:13. And led him away to Annas first; for he was father in law to Caiaphas, which was the high priest that same year.

John 18:14. Now Caiaphas was he, which gave counsel to the Jews, that it was expedient that one man should die for the people.

John 18:24. Now Annas had sent him bound unto Caiaphas the high priest.

Luke 22:54. Then took they him, and led him, and brought him into the high priest's house. And Peter followed afar off.

John 18:19. The high priest then asked Jesus of his disciples, and of his doctrine.

John 18:20. Jesus answered him, I spake openly to the world; I ever taught in the synagogue, and in the temple, whither the Jews always resort; and in secret have I said nothing.

John 18:21. Why askest thou me? ask them which heard me, what I have said unto them: behold, they know what I said.

John 18:22. And when he had thus spoken, one of the officers which stood by struck Jesus with the palm of his hand, saying, Answerest thou the high priest so?

John 18:23. Jesus answered him, If I have spoken evil, bear witness of the evil: but if well, why smitest thou me?

Matthew 26:59. Now the chief priests, and elders, and

all the council, sought false witness against Jesus, to put him to death;

Mark 14:56. For many bare false witness against him, but their witness agreed not together.

Matthew 26:60. . . . yea, though many false witnesses came, yet found they none. At the last came two false witnesses,

Mark 14:57. . . . saying,

Mark 14:58. We heard him say, I will destroy this temple that is made with hands, and within three days I will build another made without hands.

Mark 14:59. But neither so did their witness agree together.

Matthew 26:62. And the high priest arose, and said unto him, Answerest thou nothing? what is it which these witness against thee?

Matthew 26:63. But Jesus held his peace. And the high priest answered and said unto him, I adjure thee by the living God, that thou tell us whether thou be the Christ, the Son of God.

Mark 14:62. And Jesus said, I am: and ye shall see the Son of man sitting on the right hand of power, and

coming in the clouds of heaven.

Matthew 26:65. Then the high priest rent his clothes, saying, He hath spoken blasphemy; what further need have we of witnesses?

Mark 14:64. Ye have heard the blasphemy: what think ye? And they all condemned him to be guilty of death.

Luke 22:63. And the men that held Jesus mocked him, and smote him.

Mark 14:65. And some began to spit on him, and to cover his face . . .

Luke 22:64. And when they had blindfolded him, they struck him on the face, and asked him, saying, Prophesy, who is it that smote thee?

Luke 22:65. And many other things blasphemously spake they against him.

Luke 22:66. And as soon as it was day, the elders of the people and the chief priests and the scribes came together, and led him into their council, saying,

Luke 22:67. Art thou the Christ? tell us. And he said unto them, If I tell you, ye will not believe:

Luke 22:68. And if I also

ask you, ye will not answer me, nor let me go.

Luke 22:69. Hereafter shall the Son of man sit on the right hand of the power of God.

Luke 22:70. Then said they all, Art thou then the Son of God? And he said unto them, Ye say that I am.

Luke 22:71. And they said, What need we any further witness? for we ourselves have heard of his own mouth.

Luke 23:1. And the whole multitude of them arose, and led him unto Pilate.

John 18:28. Then led they Jesus from Caiaphas unto the hall of judgment: and it was early; and they themselves went not into the judgment hall, lest they should be defiled; but that they might eat the passover.

John 18:29. Pilate then went out unto them, and said, What accusation bring ye against this man?

John 18:30. They answered and said unto him, If he were not a malefactor, we would not have delivered him up unto thee.

John 18:31. Then said Pilate unto them, Take ye him, and judge him according to your law. The Jews there-fore said unto him, It is not lawful for us to put any man to death:

John 18:32. That the saying of Jesus might be fulfilled, which he spake, signifying what death he should die.

Luke 23:2. And they began to accuse him, saying, We found this fellow perverting the nation, and forbidding to give tribute to Caesar, saying that he himself is Christ a King.

John 18:33. Then Pilate entered into the judgment hall again, and called Jesus, and said unto him, Art thou the King of the Jews?

John 18:34. Jesus answered him, Sayest thou this thing of thyself, or did others tell it thee of me?

John 18:35. Pilate answered, Am I a Jew? Thine own nation and the chief priests have delivered thee unto me: what hast thou done?

John 18:36. Jesus answered, My kingdom is not of this world: if my kingdom were of this world, then would my servants fight, that I should not be delivered to the Jews: but now is my kingdom not from hence.

John 18:37. Pilate therefore said unto him, Art thou a king then? Jesus answered, Thou sayest that I am a king. To this end was I born, and for this cause came I into the world, that I should bear witness unto the truth. Every one that is of the truth heareth my voice.

John 18:38. Pilate saith unto him, What is truth? And when he had said this, he went out again unto the Jews, and saith unto them, I find in him no fault at all.

Luke 23:5. And they were the more fierce, saying, He stirreth up the people, teaching throughout all Jewry, beginning from Galilee to this place.

Luke 23:6. When Pilate heard of Galilee, he asked whether the man were a Galilaean.

Luke 23:7. And as soon as he knew that he belonged unto Herod's jurisdiction, he sent him to Herod, who himself also was at Jerusalem at that time.

Luke 23:8. And when Herod saw Jesus, he was exceeding glad: for he was desirous to see him of a long season, because he had heard many things of him; and he hoped to have seen some miracle done by him.

Luke 23:9. Then he ques-

tioned with him in many words; but he answered him nothing.

Luke 23:10. And the chief priests and scribes stood and vehemently accused him.

Luke 23:11. And Herod with his men of war set him at nought, and mocked him, and arrayed him in a gorgeous robe, and sent him again to Pilate.

Luke 23:12. And the same day Pilate and Herod were made friends together: for before they were at enmity between themselves.

Luke 23:13. And Pilate, when he had called together the chief priests and the rulers and the people,

Luke 23:14. Said unto them, Ye have brought this man unto me, as one that perverteth the people: and, behold, I, having examined him before you, have found no fault in this man touching those things whereof ye accuse him:

Luke 22:15. No, nor yet Herod: for I sent you to him; and, lo, nothing worthy of death is done unto him.

Luke 23:16. I will therefore chastise him, and release him.

John 19:7. The Jews answered him, We have a law, and by our law he ought to die, because he made himself the Son of God.

John 19:8. When Pilate therefore heard that saying, he was the more afraid;

John 19:9. And went again into the judgment hall, and saith unto Jesus, Whence art thou? But Jesus gave him no answer.

Matthew 27:13. Then said Pilate unto him, Hearest thou not how many things they witness against thee?

Matthew 27:14. And he answered him to never a word; insomuch that the governor marvelled greatly.

John 19:10. Then saith Pilate unto him, Speakest thou not unto me? knowest thou not that I have power to crucify thee, and have power to release thee?

John 19:11. Jesus answered, Thou couldest have no power at all against me, except it were given thee from above: therefore he that delivered me unto thee hath the greater sin.

John 19:12. And from thenceforth Pilate sought to release him: but the Jews cried out, saying, If thou let this man go, thou art not Caesar's friend: whosoever maketh himself a king speaketh against Caesar.

John 19:13. When Pilate therefore heard that saying, he brought Jesus forth, and sat down in the judgment seat in a place that is called the Pavement, but in the Hebrew, Gabbatha.

Matthew 27:19. When he was set down on the judgment seat, his wife sent unto him, saying, Have thou nothing to do with that just man: for I have suffered many things this day in a dream because of him.

Matthew 27:15. Now at that feast the governor was wont to release unto the people a prisoner, whom they would.

Matthew 27:16. And they had then a notable prisoner, called Barabbas.

Mark 15:7. . . . which lay bound with them that had made insurrection with him, who had committed murder in the insurrection.

Luke 23:19. (Who for a certain sedition made in the city, and for murder, was cast into prison.)

Matthew 27:17. Therefore when they were gathered together, Pilate said unto them, Whom will ye that I release unto you? Barabbas, or Jesus which is called Christ?

Matthew 27:18. For he knew that for envy they had delivered him.

John 18:39. But ye have a custom, that I should release unto you one at the passover: will ye therefore that I release unto you the King of the Jews?

Matthew 27:20. But the chief priests and elders persuaded the multitude that they should ask Barabbas, and destroy Jesus.

Matthew 27:21. The governor answered and said unto them, Whether of the twain will ye that I release unto you? They said, Barabbas.

Mark 15:12. And Pilate answered and said again unto them, What will ye then that I shall do unto him whom ye call the King of the Jews?

Matthew 27:22. Pilate saith unto them, What shall I do then with Jesus which is called Christ? They all say unto him, Let him be crucified.

Matthew 27:23. And the governor said, Why, what evil hath he done? But they cried out the more, saying, Let him be crucified.

Matthew 27:24. When Pilate saw that he could prevail nothing, but that rather a tumult was made, he took water, and washed his hands before the multitude, saying, I am innocent of the blood of this just person: see ye to it.

Matthew 27:25. Then answered all the people, and said, His blood be on us, and on our children.

Mark 15:15. And so Pilate, willing to content the people, released Barabbas unto them, and delivered Jesus . . .

Luke 23:25. And he released unto them him that for sedition and murder was cast into prison, whom they had desired; but he delivered Jesus to their will.

Mark 15:16. And the soldiers led him away into the hall, called Praetorium; and they call together the whole band.

John 19:1. Then Pilate therefore took Jesus, and scourged him.

John 19:2. And the soldiers platted a crown of thorns, and put it on his head, and they put on him a purple robe,

John 19:3. And said, Hail, King of the Jews! and they smote him with their hands.

Mark 15:19. And they smote him on the head with a reed, and did spit upon him, and bowing their knees worshipped him.

Mark 15:20. And when they had mocked him, they took off the purple from him, and put his own clothes on him, and led him out . . .

Luke 23:20. Pilate therefore, willing to release Jesus, spake again to them.

Luke 23:21. But they cried, saying, Crucify him, crucify him.

Luke 23:22. And he said unto them the third time, Why, what evil hath he done? I have found no cause of death in him: I will therefore chastise him, and let him go.

John 19:14. And it was the preparation of the passover, and about the sixth hour: and he saith unto the Jews, Behold your King!

John 19:15. But they cried out, Away with him, away with him, crucify him. Pilate saith unto them, Shall I crucify your King? The chief priests answered, We have no king but Caesar.

John 19:16. Then delivered he him therefore unto them to be crucified. And they took Jesus, and led him away.

Luke 23:24. And Pilate gave sentence that it should be as they required.

Cross-references

Matthew 26:57–68; 27:1–2, 11–31   Mark 14:53–65; 15:1–20
Luke 22:54, 63–71; 23:1–25
John 18:12–15, 28–40; 19:1–15

Christ's trials were conducted by two separate groups of authorities. The first two trials were conducted by his own people —the rulers of the Jews who had looked forward to his coming. Ironically, he was tried and condemned by them for claiming to be what he was—the Messiah.

The third trial was conducted under the authority of Rome and consisted of a sequence of hearings before Pilate and also the "interview of silence" before Herod. Herod was the tetrarch appointed by Rome to rule the province of Galilee, from which Jesus came. His attempted interview was much like the one held before Caiaphas, and he did not try the Savior nor condemn him.

Pilate was the ruler of the Roman Empire in Judea. He was a heathen, concerned only with the protection of the Empire and of his own position. He came to his position of authority shortly before the ministry of John the Baptist[4] and was therefore the principal Roman authority during Jesus' entire ministry.

The records indicate that Jesus was taken from place to place during the night of his trials, an easy thing to do since all of the principal participants in his trials either lived in Jerusalem or took up residence there during the Passover festival.

From the Garden of Gethsemane, Christ was first taken to the palace of Annas, which was located between the upper city and the Tyropoeon. The Tyropoeon, known as the "valley of the cheese mongers," connected the eastern and western hills of the city.[5] The scriptures record that a Roman guard[6] accompanied Christ from the Garden of Gethsemane to the palace of Annas,[7] but at this point he seems to have been turned over to the temple guard, for the Gospels do not mention the Romans again until the crucifixion. Christ was next taken to Caiaphas in the palace of the high priest, which was located on the northeastern corner of Mount Zion.[8] This is undoubtedly the place where the Sanhedrists assembled to try the Lord.[9] The palace was on the slope of the mount and had a lower story positioned beneath the principal living apartments, which had a porch in front (wherein Peter walked): the porch was described as being "beneath in the palace."[10]

After the trials were finished at the palace of Caiaphas, the crowd took the bound and brutalized Savior and wound their way up the upper city's narrow streets to Pilate in the palace of Herod.[11] Pilate did not usually reside in Jerusalem, but he always came there during this particular feast so that he could be on hand to control any potential uprisings. There were two living quarters available to him in Jerusalem: the first was in the Fortress of Antonia, and the second was in the palace of Herod the Great. It is unlikely that he chose the fortress, because it also contained the rough barracks where the Roman soldiers were stationed. He probably stayed in Herod's magnificent palace, which was located at the northwestern angle of the upper city.[12] The residence of the Roman governor, wherever he was staying, was always called the Praetorium.

Because Pilate, the Roman heathen, was living in Herod's palace, the Jews would not enter for fear of Levitical uncleanness during the Passover celebration.[13] During the discussions there

Pilate discovered that Jesus was a Galilean. For some reason, perhaps to relieve himself of the obligation of judging the Savior, Pilate sent him on to King Herod (son of Herod the Great and current ruler of Galilee and Perea). Herod always came to the Feast of the Passover, and while there he occupied the palace of the Maccabees (which was close to that of Caiaphas). After the "interview of silence" before Herod, Christ was once again marched back through the same streets to the palace of Herod the Great to be judged by Pilate, where he was first condemned and then marched to the outer gates of the city and thence to Golgotha.

The Law

As already discussed, the Jewish leaders had one goal — to condemn Christ in such a manner that the Romans would execute him immediately.[14] The Jews were forced to enlist the aid of the Romans because the Sanhedrin did not have the authority to enforce the death sentence[15] (even though they would later illegally do so in the case of Stephen; see Acts 6–7). Although they levied various capital charges against the Lord, the Sanhedrists were unable to convict him until he himself provided them with the evidence they needed to condemn him under Jewish law. This evidence was derived from a question the high priest asked Jesus: "Art thou then the Son of God?" And the Lord replied that he was. The answer tore at the very foundations of contemporary Judaism, and the high priest immediately rent his clothes, suspended all of the feigned compliance with rules of Jewish law, and called for a vote of condemnation from the Sanhedrists.

While the charge of blasphemy was a capital offense in Judaism, Roman law did not consider it as such. The Jewish leadership had to cleverly manipulate the evidence so that the charge became that of a capital offense to Rome — treason.

Although the Sanhedrists outwardly complied with many of their legal requirements, they blatantly ignored established legal proceedings in order to obtain their desired ambition. Haste was the rule![16] Their laws demanded justice, but their actions displayed ruthless revenge.

The Jewish system of justice at the time contained the following legal requirements, each of which was violated during the Savior's trials:

1. It was unlawful for the Sanhedrin to sit at night to consider any capital charge, nor could they consider the same on the Sabbath, any feast day, or the eve of any feast day.[17]

2. A defendant was regarded as innocent until proven guilty.

3. No one could be tried or condemned in absentia.

4. Their high, moral law demanded that in all capital offense trials they should remember the value of human life.

5. Accusers were to appear in person and were to be warned against bearing false witness. (During Jesus' trial, the Sanhedrists and the chief priest actively sought false witnesses.)

6. The accused was not to be left undefended, and the person or group defending the accused was to work diligently for the acquittal.

7. Any and all evidence that was favorable to the defendant was to be freely admitted before the trying body.

8. No member of the court would vote for condemnation once he had spoken in favor of acquittal.

9. When the trying body voted, the youngest members voted first so that they would not be influenced by their elders.

10. In a capital charge, the vote in favor of death had to be by a majority of at least two.

11. If a guilty vote was decided upon, it had to be officially taken the day following the trial.

12. No criminal trial could be carried on throughout the night.

13. No judgment recommending death could be rendered without the Sanhedrin fasting the entire day before the sentence was given.

14. No one could be executed on the same day their sentence was pronounced.[18]

15. The Law and tradition demanded that a second full hearing and trial be given when capital punishment was imposed.[19]

16. All capital charge trials must be held in the official courtroom of the Sanhedrin.[20]

17. A unanimous vote of guilty was not enforceable.

Although the Lord was personally interviewed by both Caiaphas and Annas, these were not official trials. Undoubtedly the interviews were held (1) to see how vigorously the Lord would defend the charges brought against him, (2) to allow time for enough Sanhedrists to be gathered at the palace of the high priest that the facade of an actual trial could be presented, and (3) to see if any of the Lord's disciples would defend him.

Once the Jewish leadership had been assembled, the Lord would have been placed before them in a standing position — directly in front of the high priest. The Sanhedrists would have been seated both to the left and to the right of the high priest in a semicircle, with a scribe at the end of each side of the semicircle to record the sentence. The accused would have been guarded by bailiffs or temple guards, while a small number of court assistants would have stood directly behind the Sanhedrists to call witnesses and carry out the court's decisions.[21]

Jesus' arrest, interviews, and trials were in violation of Jewish law at the time. Any semblance of legality was trampled under the feet of the Jewish rulers in their rush to be rid of the Savior. (An excellent work on the trials of Jesus from a legal standpoint was done by Walter M. Chandler in 1925. For details the reader is referred to that work and the citations therein.[22])

To say that the trials of Jesus were not in accordance with Jewish law is an understatement, but it should be clearly understood that such was *not* the purpose of the high priest and the Sanhedrists — to try the Lord in the ordinary way and to give him a fair trial would have ensured his acquittal. Instead, they presented a facade of a trial to justify their actions before the people, particularly those attending the Passover feast, and to specifically impress the Roman leader, Pilate, so that they could enlist the Roman judicial system (which they needed to carry out the sentence of death), for they had no power to enforce their wrongful verdict. The outcome of their mock trial was predetermined: throughout the Lord's ministry they had wanted to kill him, and it became their avowed intention after he raised Lazarus from the dead (John 11:53).

Neither the chief judge nor the Sanhedrists could bring charges against an accused; they could only adjudicate the charges.[23] The person who initiated the charge acted as the prosecuting witness (they would also have been the executioner in the case of the death penalty); no record of any kind of an "official" prosecutor is found in Israel's history.[24] When Christ was arraigned, however, no individual came forth to formally charge him. All of the charges were made by the high priest, and false witnesses were brought forward in an attempt to accuse him, but they failed miserably.

They could not charge him with deliberately breaking the Sabbath, for it would raise the question of his miracles, which had been unquestionably documented. They could not charge him with secret doctrinal teachings, for he had taught openly in both the synagogues and the temple. They could not bring charges against him because of the actions of his disciples, for he had successfully refuted their accusations concerning the Twelve (see Mark 2:23–28). Finally, knowing that he had claimed on many occasions to be the long-awaited Messiah, the high priest asked the Lord if he was, indeed, the Son of God, to which Jesus simply answered yes. Then, rather than determining whether he was the Son of God under any system of justice, they reached the foregone conclusion that he was not and that he had blasphemed: their justification for his condemnation thus came from his own mouth.

A second mock trial was held for the sole purpose of again seeming to comply with correct legal procedure, for Jewish law demanded that two trials be held when capital punishment had been imposed. This time the Sanhedrists wanted only to determine whether the Lord had in fact claimed the Messiahship. Again he affirmed his divine Sonship, and again the Sanhedrists unanimously condemned him. Then they sent him to Pilate.

Throughout Israel's history the Jews had been meticulously just in their legal procedure. They had developed a justice system which protected the rights of the accused, and they prided themselves on their fairness —but on this night, for this Man, there was no justice.

The Jewish Trials and Peter's Denials

Matthew 26:69–75

69. Now Peter sat without in the palace: and a damsel came unto him, saying, Thou also wast with Jesus of Galilee.

70. But he denied before them all, saying, I know not what thou sayest.

71. And when he was gone out into the porch, another maid saw him, and said unto them that were there, This fellow was also with Jesus of Nazareth.

72. And again he denied

with an oath, I do not know the man.

73. And after a while came unto him they that stood by, and said to Peter, Surely thou also art one of them; for thy speech bewrayeth thee.

74. Then began he to curse and to answer, saying, I know not the man. And immediately the cock crew.

75. And Peter remembered the word of Jesus, which said unto him, Before the cock crow, thou shalt deny me thrice. And he went out, and wept bitterly.

Cross-references

Mark 14:66–72   Luke 22:55–62
John 18:16–27

After Jesus' arrest late on Thursday evening, perhaps between 11:00 P.M. and midnight, he was taken to the palace of Annas, the father-in-law of Caiaphas, the high priest. How long Annas interrogated Christ is not known. By the time Peter and John caught up with the Savior the interview with Annas was over, and the temple guard was probably in the process of leading Jesus to Caiaphas for trial. The two Apostles followed the Lord and his captors. John was known to the high priest and went unimpeded into the palace, but Peter could not gain access and John had to return to the door to help him get in. John apparently went on into the inner rooms to observe the trial, while Peter was required to stay in the outer courtyard, or porch area, where a fire had been built to warm the guards while they waited.

Caiaphas held a personal interview with Jesus prior to the commencement of the first trial. Perhaps this interview was held to allow time for the Sanhedrists to assemble, or perhaps Caiaphas was interested in determining the strength of the Lord's defense. The old charges that had been levied against the Lord during his ministry were not pursued. "His violations of the Sabbath, as they called them, were all connected with miracles, and brought them, therefore, upon dangerous ground. His rejection of oral tradition involved a question on which Sadducees and Pharisees were at deadly feud. His authoritative cleansing of the Temple might be regarded with favour both by the Rabbis and the people."[25] Therefore, the first charges brought by Caiaphas concerned the Lord's disciples and his doctrine.

Caiaphas's intent, as already mentioned, was to convict Jesus on a charge punishable by death, not only under Jewish law, but under the Roman law as well. The charges concerning the Lord's disciples and his doctrine were aimed at (1) unorthodox teaching, which might be construed as heresy and therefore punishable by death under Jewish law, and (2) secret seditions, which were punishable by death under Roman law.[26]

The Lord passed over the question concerning his disciples (perhaps to relieve them of any involvement in his arrest and trial) and defended the charge concerning his doctrine by declaring, "I spake openly to the world; I ever taught in the synagogue, and in the temple," the normal teaching forums for the Jews. He did not need to defend his teachings — they were not heretical or apostate — so he suggested that the high priest "ask them which heard me, what I have said unto them: behold they know what I said." The answer offended one of the officers watching Jesus, and he struck the Lord with the palm of his hand stating, "Answerest thou the high priest so?" But Jesus was right, and the high priest and the officer were wrong. The Lord responded, "If I have spoken evil, bear witness of the evil: but if well, why smitest thou me?" It was another reminder to his persecutors of his rights under Jewish law.

No further information is recorded of the conversation between Caiaphas and Jesus, and there is no indication of how long the Lord was questioned prior to the arrival of the Sanhedrists for the first of the officially required "trials" — perhaps another hour or more lapsed before the formal trials began. However, it would seem probable that Peter's first denial took place during this lull.

When Peter first boldly entered the courtyard of Caiaphas' palace, he was venturing into the lair of his Lord's most bitter enemies. He sat down by a fire to warm himself on the chilly April night, even though he was in the midst of the servants and the guards of the very men who would sit in judgment upon the Savior. A maid who was employed as the door-portress moved to the fire and fixed her attention on Peter. She apparently recognized him from some prior meeting, and accused him of being with Jesus in Galilee. The Gospels disagree as to what exactly she said. John records that she accused Peter of being a disciple, while the other writers only state that she accused him of "being with Jesus." In the Garden of Gethsemane apparently Peter's fear for his safety had overcome the love he held for his Master, and he had fled into the night with the other ten Apostles. Now, he was again caught off guard. Fear swelled within him as he denied knowing the Savior. For the moment his denial was accepted, and he left the fire for the safety of the porch, where he could be alone.

While Peter waited, the Sanhedrists began arriving for the Lord's first formal trial. Perhaps less than half of the official body[27] had assembled when the trial began. They had sent for false witnesses to fortify the charges that had been levied by Caiaphas, but time was short and their preparation was inadequate; thus, the witnesses could not agree on their testimonies. Relentlessly, the court continued to feign legality by calling other false witnesses in an attempt to convict the Lord, but they could not find any who could support the charges. Finally, two witnesses came forth to falsely testify against Jesus concerning his prophecy on the destruction of the temple. The Lord had spoken symbolically of his body and its resurrection when he had talked of the temple being destroyed and raised up again, but in an effort to create a charge that would stand up under Jewish and Roman law, the judges perverted his meaning so that it appeared that he was threatening to destroy the temple building itself—but even then the witnesses' testimonies did not agree.

The Lord had conversed with Caiaphas before the trials started, but while false testimony was being borne against him Jesus remained silent, refusing to dignify his enemies' collusion with a reply. Finally, the high priest stood and asked the Lord why he had not answered the charges of the witnesses. The Lord again remained silent. In desperation the high priest commanded Jesus "by the living God" to speak. Obviously, the question in point did not concern any of the charges previously levied against him, nor did it concern the false testimony being presented. Throughout his ministry the Lord had laid claim to the Messiahship; during the good shepherd discourse he had been asked plainly to tell them if he was the Christ, and they had rejected his answer (John 10:24). Now, as he stood before the elders, the chief priests, and the members of the Sanhedrin, Caiaphas again asked, "Tell us whether thou be the Christ, the Son of God."

The Lord broke his silence and in quiet majesty said, "I am: and ye shall see the Son of man sitting on the right hand of power, and coming in the clouds of heaven." This was too much for Caiaphas: he did that which was forbidden under Jewish law and rent his clothes (Leviticus 10:6; 21:10), condemned Jesus for blasphemy, rejected all the witnesses, and called for the Savior's death. The Sanhedrists followed suit, and all pronounced the sentence of death upon Christ. The first trial was over.

During this time Peter had been on the porch in the courtyard, undoubtedly listening intently to the proceedings of the trial. He was cold, perhaps not just from the night air but also chilled by the reality of his Lord's condemnation. Some time had passed, perhaps as much as two hours or so, and he moved from the security of the porch area back toward the fire's warmth. His movement was again noticed by the door-portress, and as he drew near to the fire he was accosted and accused a second time of being one of Jesus' followers. Again he denied the accusation but this time did so with an oath, as if to emphasize his "innocence" and protect himself from further confrontation.

The Lord was condemned to death for blasphemy, a heinous crime against the God of Israel; and as if the sentence of death was not enough, some in the hall verbally and physically vented their anger and hatred upon the Savior, for they now considered him to be a false prophet.[28] They mocked him and spat upon him and, after blindfolding him, struck him on the face, blasphemously taunting him: "Prophesy, who is it that smote thee?" How long the Lord was treated in this inhuman manner is unknown, but his sentencing and the derision could have extended throughout another hour of that fateful morning.

Finally, the Savior was brought before the Sanhedrists for his second "trial." This trial no doubt took place in the same hall as the first, the only change being that additional leaders probably had arrived to help sit in judgment. Meanwhile, Peter's activities were reaching a climax in the courtyard.

Nothing is recorded of the conversation that was probably taking place among the excited servants and guards as they stood around the fire and observed the progress of the trial and the vehement punishment Christ was receiving. Peter undoubtedly took part in their conversation, because one stated, "Surely thou also art one of them; for thy speech bewrayeth [reveals] thee." Perhaps the Lord's initial punishment was over and a pause took place in the proceedings. In any case, Peter was again accused of being one of the Lord's disciples. It appears that despite Peter's previous denials and oaths, he was still a suspect to the highly stimulated crowd milling about the courtyard. At last one of them, a kinsman of Malchus, whose ear Peter had struck, charged him: not only did the man accuse Peter of being a disciple, but he also claimed that Peter had been with Jesus in the Garden at the time of Christ's arrest, and as if to prove his accusation, the man claimed that Peter's Galilean dialect proved it.

Others joined in the damaging charges, and Peter was once again faced with the fear of detection and perhaps physical harm. He began to "curse and to swear, saying, I know not this man of whom ye speak." At that fateful moment the cock crew, and the Lord, standing in the upper hall where he could observe what was taking place, turned and looked down upon Peter. Peter's gaze met his Lord's and the memory of the Lord's prophecy overcame him. Leaving the palace in the depths of humility and despair, he "wept bitterly."

Let no one accuse Peter of denying that Jesus was the Christ — he claimed only to not know this man of whom they spoke. His denials were precipitated out of fear, fear compounded by the dreadful actions taking place to the very Christ he had associated with and loved for three long years. Peter was the first man to proclaim Christ as the Messiah: he had walked upon the water to him, had indignantly affirmed that he would rather die than deny him, and had courageously drawn his sword in the Lord's defense. Peter's "so-called denial of his Lord . . . was rather a failure to stand up and testify of the divine Sonship" when the opportunity presented itself among his enemies and not a "denial of any divinity resident in the Son of Man."[29]

The Lord's second trial before the Sanhedrists probably began somewhere between 5:00 A.M. and 6:00 A.M. Friday. No longer was an attempt made to feign legalities. The sole question before the court at this point concerned Christ's claim to the Messiahship. "Art thou the Christ?" they asked again, and the Lord's response

reflected the blind attitude of the Jewish leaders and others of the
chosen people: "If I tell you, ye will not believe," he said, nor
would they have responded to his questions if he were to attempt
to verify his claim. Again he testified of his divinity, his answer af-
firming their question, but the court persisted and again asked,
"Art thou then the Son of God?" The Lord again responded, "Ye
say that I am." The trial was over; they had no need for further
witnesses for they had "heard of his own mouth." He who was the
Son of God had affirmed that relationship. Bound and condemned, the Savior of the world was next led to the heathen court
of Pontius Pilate.

The Roman Trial

At around 7:00 A.M., the Lord was taken to Pilate. This was
the day of the Passover, and the same Jewish leaders who had
thirsted "for innocent blood" throughout the night would not
enter Pilate's heathen hall for fear of the "mere proximity of
leaven."[30] Pilate had probably been told of the coming delegation
for he was waiting for them in the judgment hall. However, since
they would not enter his palace because of the feast, he came out
to them. He had undoubtedly heard of Jesus and the potential
problems that his ministry had created, but he also recognized that
the Savior was being delivered to him by some very envious
Jewish rulers[31] (Mark 15:10). Pilate asked the Jews what Christ was
accused of, and his question seemed to frustrate them. In their
frenzied hatred of the Lord, they had apparently not anticipated
that they would have to provide justification for the death
sentence they had levied against him. Their response to Pilate was
not convincing: "If he were not a malefactor, we would not have
delivered him up unto thee." Pilate, however, told them to take
care of the judgment themselves (perhaps in spite since he felt great
animosity for the Jews). But they could not put Christ to death!

The Jewish leaders were confronted with the fact that they
must change the charge against Jesus from blasphemy to treason —
from a religious violation to a civil one — so again they falsely
accused him. Jesus had perverted the nation, had forbidden the
giving of tribute to Caesar, and had made himself a king, they
claimed. Pilate listened to the charges and then asked Jesus, "Art

thou the King of the Jews?" "Thou sayest it," was the Lord's immediate response.

Perhaps irritated that the matter had not been easily resolved, Pilate entered the judgment hall and had Jesus brought before him. Again he put the question to him, "Art thou the King of the Jews?" Jesus answered the question with a question, for he wanted to know the background of this Roman's query. "Sayest thou this thing of thyself," he asked, "or did others tell it thee of me?" Pilate's answer showed his lack of understanding of the Messianic mission and his distaste for the Israelites. "Am I a Jew?" he contemptuously responded.

The Lord then answered Pilate's first question, matching his answer to the Roman's understanding by testifying that his kingdom was not of the world, for if it were his servants would have fought for him at the time of his arrest. Pilate persisted, "Art thou a king then?" "To this end was I born," the Lord responded. His answer would only have meaning to those who understood the truth of who he really was, and he explained that those who sought that truth would receive it. Pilate was not interested in the religious beliefs of the Jews, however, so he ended the conversation with the dialectic, "What is truth?" Having determined that Jesus was no threat to him or Rome, he returned to the waiting crowd and pronounced that he had found no fault in the Lord worthy of Roman justice: thus, he acquitted Christ of the Roman charges.

The Jewish rulers would not, could not, allow this to be their answer. They continued to accuse Christ, and as they argued before Pilate, blasphemy turned into civil unrest and finally became treason, "beginning from Galilee to this place." Pilate suddenly recognized a potential escape from his problems with these unwieldy subjects: if the man was from Galilee he "belonged unto Herod's jurisdiction," so he sent him to King Herod, who was also in Jerusalem for the feast.

Herod was residing in the old palace of the Asmoneans near Pilate in the palace of Herod the Great,[32] and when word spread of Pilate's actions, the crowd (swollen with visitors and citizens alike) swarmed[33] through the streets of the upper city to follow Jesus, bound and heavily guarded, to Herod's abode.[34] Herod had been

warned that Christ was coming and was exceedingly glad to see
him "because he had heard many things of him; and he hoped to
have seen some miracle done by him." Herod questioned Jesus at
length, but the Lord maintained silence before him. The "interview
of silence" was brief, leaving Herod's desires unsatisfied, and the
chief priests and scribes soon started vehemently accusing Jesus
again. Perhaps to ingratiate himself to these religious rulers who
hated him, Herod commanded his men of war to mock the Lord,
and after they had finished ridiculing him they clothed him in a
"gorgeous robe" and returned him to Pilate.

Pilate was told of Herod's "interview of silence" and determined that Herod had also found no guilt in Christ. Pilate called
the Jewish rulers together and informed them that neither he nor
Herod had found fault with Jesus; therefore, he would merely
chastise and release him. This was Christ's second acquittal under
Roman law.

Frustrated at their inability to successfully negotiate the charge
of treason, the Jewish rulers now testified that the Lord must die
because he had "made himself the Son of God." Pilate was
superstitious, and this claim made him "afraid." Again he entered
the judgment hall and brought Jesus before him. He questioned the
Lord concerning his origin, but the Savior did not answer. Pilate
reiterated the charges and the accusations that had been brought
against Jesus by his own people, but still the Lord did not respond,
causing Pilate to marvel. Finally, Pilate threatened the Lord, em-
phasizing his power to release or crucify him. To this the Lord
responded, but not, perhaps, as Pilate had expected: he testified
that Pilate could harm him only if that power "were given thee
from above," and then the Lord uttered a judgment before Pilate,
indicating that the greater sin for the results of this day would be
on his accusers, not on his executioner. Pilate's fears increased,
and perhaps he *was* less guilty than the Jewish rulers, for at this
point he was anxious to spare the Savior's life.[35]

Pilate again presented the Lord to the chief priests and the
rulers and advised leniency, but they shouted, "Away with this
man." By now they had devised a scheme that would force Pilate
to give in to their demands. "If thou let this man go, thou art not

Caesar's friend," they cried. This statement put Pilate's political position in jeopardy. He could see that the Jews were not going to yield, so he returned to the judgment seat and again had Jesus brought before him. At this point a strange occurrence took place that would have only fueled the fires of Pilate's superstition. His wife sent him a message: she had had a dream concerning Jesus, and, although nothing is recorded of the context of the dream, it had obviously upset her. She warned her husband to beware of the sentence he pronounced, for Jesus, she wrote, was a "just man."

Pilate found himself in an untenable situation. Obviously Christ had done nothing worthy of death and his superstitious nature made him fear the consequences of his wife's dream; on the other hand, if his Jewish subjects rioted he would incur the wrath of Rome. To rid himself of his problems he fell back on an old Roman custom: Rome always released a prisoner at the feast of the Passover to show its "benevolence" to the people of Palestine. He selected for this purpose one Barabbas, a notable prisoner that had been convicted of treason, murder, and insurrection. He had him brought forth and stood him next to Jesus so that the people could choose the man they wanted released. Pilate probably felt that the people would choose to release Jesus rather than have a recognized murderer back in their midst, and he was surprised when the Jews shouted for the release of Barabbas and continued to demand the crucifixion of Christ.

Recognizing that the situation was beyond his control, Pilate appeared before the multitude and washed his hands, symbolically ridding himself of the blood of the "just person" they were so eager to destroy. "All the people" recognized the meaning of the gesture from their traditions (Deuteronomy 21:1-9; Psalms 26:6; 73:13) and readily accepted the guilt for the death of their Messiah, screaming, "His blood be on us, and on our children."

"It was fitting that *they*, who had preferred an abject Sadducee to their True Priest, and an incestuous Idumaean to their Lord and King, should deliberately prefer a murderer to their Messiah."[36]

An astonished Pilate remonstrated, "What will ye then that I shall do unto him whom ye call the King of the Jews?" "Crucify him!" was the violent response. In dismay Pilate cried out, "Why, what evil hath he done?" But the cries grew louder and more vehement, "Let him be crucified." Pilate, a weak man who was fearful of another riot, yielded to their demands:[37] he released Barabbas and sentenced Jesus to death.

Yet one more cruelty would be inflicted upon the Lord prior to his crucifixion: Pilate released him to his soldiers, who took him into the Praetorium and "scourged him." Scourging was inflicted by striking the condemned person with a whip "loaded with lead, or armed with spikes and bones, which lacerated back, and chest, and face, till the victim sometimes fell down before the judge a bleeding mass of torn flesh."[38] The soldiers also beat the Savior with their hands and with reeds, and they spat upon him and forced a crown of plaited thorns upon his head. After placing a purple robe on his bleeding back and shoulders, they mocked him and hailed him as the "king" of the Jews, and, in blasphemous irreverence, they bowed before him. Finally, they replaced the regal robe with his own clothing and took him back to Pilate, who once more appealed to the mercy of the raging multitude. He was yet willing to release Christ, but the multitude would have none of it, and they screamed over and over, "Crucify him, crucify him." They were in a frenzy, and the only thing that would sate their fury was the blood of their Messiah!

In the face of their anger Pilate still pleaded for Christ, testifying that Jesus had done no evil and that he should only be chastised and then released. He again presented the Lord to them crying, "Behold your King." But the rulers and the multitude were past all reason and shouted, "Away with him, crucify him. Shall I crucify your King?" Pilate asked again. "We have no king but Caesar," was the instant response. Pilate had no other recourse: he gave the order, and the Savior of the world —the Messiah the chosen people had anticipated in all that they did and the King for whom they had waited for centuries —was led away to be crucified.

"It Is Finished"

8

The Crucifixion

Matthew 27:32–66

32. And as they came out, they found a man of Cyrene, Simon by name: him they compelled to bear his cross.

33. And when they were come unto a place called Golgotha, that is to say, a place of a skull,

34. They gave him vinegar to drink mingled with gall: and when he had tasted thereof, he would not drink.

35. And they crucified him, and parted his garments, casting lots: that it might be fulfilled which was spoken by the prophet, They parted my garments among them, and upon my vesture did they cast lots.

36. And sitting down they watched him there;

37. And set up over his head his accusation written, THIS IS JESUS THE KING OF THE JEWS.

38. Then were there two thieves crucified with him, one on the right hand, and another on the left.

39. And they that passed by reviled him, wagging their heads,

40. And saying, Thou that

destroyest the temple, and buildest it in three days, save thyself. If thou be the Son of God, come down from the cross.

41. Likewise also the chief priests mocking him, with the scribes and elders, said,

42. He saved others; himself he cannot save. If he be the King of Israel, let him now come down from the cross, and we will believe him.

43. He trusted in God; let him deliver him now, if he will have him: for he said, I am the Son of God.

44. The thieves also, which were crucified with him, cast the same in his teeth.

45. Now from the sixth hour there was darkness over all the land unto the ninth hour.

46. And about the ninth hour Jesus cried with a loud voice, saying, Eli, Eli, lama sabachthani? that is to say, My God, my God, why hast thou forsaken me?

47. Some of them that stood there, when they heard that, said, This man calleth for Elias.

48. And straightway one of them ran, and took a sponge, and filled it with vinegar, and put it on a reed, and gave him to drink.

49. The rest said, Let be, let us see whether Elias will come to save him.

50. Jesus, when he had cried again with a loud voice, yielded up the ghost.

51. And, behold, the veil of the temple was rent in twain from the top to the bottom; and the earth did quake, and the rocks rent;

52. And the graves were opened; and many bodies of the saints which slept arose,

53. And came out of the graves after his resurrection, and went into the holy city, and appeared unto many.

54. Now when the centurion, and they that were with him, watching Jesus, saw the earthquake, and those things that were done, they feared greatly, saying, Truly this was the Son of God.

55. And many women were there beholding afar off, which followed Jesus from Galilee, ministering unto him:

56. Among which was Mary Magdalene, and Mary the mother of James and Joses, and the mother of Zebedee's children.

57. When the even was

come, there came a rich man of Arimathaea, named Joseph, who also himself was Jesus' disciple:

58. He went to Pilate, and begged the body of Jesus. Then Pilate commanded the body to be delivered.

59. And when Joseph had taken the body, he wrapped it in a clean linen cloth,

60. And laid it in his own new tomb, which he had hewn out in the rock: and he rolled a great stone to the door of the sepulchre, and departed.

61. And there was Mary Magdalene, and the other Mary, sitting over against the sepulchre.

62. Now the next day, that followed the day of the preparation, the chief priests and Pharisees came together unto Pilate,

63. Saying, Sir, we remember that that deceiver said, while he was yet alive, After three days I will rise again.

64. Command therefore that the sepulchre be made sure until the third day, lest his disciples come by night, and steal him away, and say unto the people, He is risen from the dead: so the last error shall be worse than the first.

65. Pilate said unto them, Ye have a watch: go your way, make it as sure as ye can.

66. So they went, and made the sepulchre sure, sealing the stone, and setting a watch.

Cross-references

Mark 15:20–47   Luke 23:26–56
John 19:16–42

The Gospel writers differ considerably on the facts and circumstances surrounding Jesus' crucifixion, and it seems apparent that John is the only one who was an eyewitness to the occurrence; however, a close reading of John's Gospel indicates that he was present during only portions of the crucifixion, performing certain errands which took him away from the cross from time to time.[1] The other Gospel writers seem to have acquired their information about the crucifixion from interviews with other eyewitnesses.[2]

After Pilate sentenced the Lord to death, the Roman soldiers savagely scourged him. Had custom been followed, two days would have elapsed between the sentencing and the execution,[3] but it is apparent that after the scourging they immediately took the Lord to be crucified (at approximately nine on Friday morning). The interviews, trials, beatings, and conveyance between palaces had taken up the entire night.

It was the Roman practice to routinely assign four soldiers to each condemned prisoner and his cross. Their job was to escort the convict through the streets to the place of execution and to sit as sentries at the crucifixion until the prisoner's death. The Romans first used crucifixion on a cross in Palestine after Caesar's death, but it was not a Jewish mode of execution. Jewish executions were usually performed by strangulation, beheading, burning, or stoning.[4]

The cross was a simple structure made of roughhewn wood.[5] Three types of crosses were commonly used: one was in the shape of the capital letter X and became known as the Saint Andrew's cross; the second was in the form of the capital letter T (the victim was attached to the horizontal part of the cross while the cross lay upon the ground, then it was lifted up and dropped into a hole which held it in an upright position); the third cross, and probably the one used for the crucifixion of Jesus, was known as the Latin cross, because the horizontal bar was attached below the top of the vertical bar. (Christ's "title" was attached to his cross above his head. This information helps to identify the type of cross used in his crucifixion.[6])

Crucifixion was a cruel method of death, each phase being designed to inflict the maximum amount of pain and suffering. Even the scourging done prior to the actual crucifixion at times caused the condemned's premature death.[7] If still alive, the prisoner was then tied to the transverse bar of his cross and required to carry it through the city streets to the place of his execution; however, there is no evidence to indicate whether the Savior was tied to his cross during this agonizing journey.

The destination of this gruesome procession for the Messiah was Golgotha, or Calvary, interpreted as the "place of a skull," or "skull." It was located near the city but outside its gates. Its exact location is not currently known (although it was probably well known at the time of Christ's death for it was undoubtedly a recognized place of execution). It was not a hill, nor is it described as such in the scriptures —it is merely called "a place."[8] Although much has been written concerning its location, "in all probability, the actual spot lies buried and obliterated under the mountainous rubbish-heaps of the ten-times-taken city."[9]

The prisoners that were to be crucified would normally have been led down the longest possible route through the city in order to punish them further and to terrorize the spectators; but on this occasion, with the Jewish Sabbath rapidly approaching, a shorter course may have been taken, with the procession exiting Jerusalem through the north (Damascus) Gate.[10]

The preceding night had taxed the Savior's strength; he had not slept or partaken of any nourishment. He was further weakened by the cruel beatings and scourging, as well as the overwhelming physical, spiritual, and emotional drain of suffering in the Garden of Gethsemane prior to his arrest. All of this had weakened him to the point that he could not physically support the crossbar's weight as he moved through the streets of Jerusalem.[11]

The guards had previously shown Jesus no mercy, and there is no reason to assume that they would do so now; but his weakness undoubtedly slowed the procession, so one Simon, a Cyrenian, was pressed into service and forced to carry Christ's crossbar to Golgotha. (Simon was probably not a disciple, but it is assumed that he and his family later became followers of the Messiah; Mark 15:21; Romans 16:13.)[12]

If custom had been followed, Christ would have been strapped to his crossbar, and perhaps it was at this moment, while the bar was removed from his shoulders and tied upon Simon's, that the episode concerning a warning to the women of Israel took place. In the crowd that was following the procession were some women who were loudly wailing and lamenting over Jesus. In all probability their laments were not for the fate of the Son of God, but were in pity and sympathy for his tortured appearance and obvious suffering.[13] Christ had triumphantly entered Jerusalem just a few days before and had paused during his entry to weep for the holy city and its daughters (Luke 19:41): now they were weeping for him. Jesus turned to the lamenting women and spoke to them, telling them not to weep for him, but for themselves and for their children—another warning of the devastating destruction and the great sorrow that would soon befall the Jews in Jerusalem. Christ told them that the days were coming when they would wish they had never had children and would beg the mountains to fall on them so their sufferings might be relieved. He referred to himself as a "green tree," for as the true Messiah he had brought the living gospel to them (although they had rejected his message). If the green tree was allowed to suffer so severely, what great sufferings would come upon them (the dry tree) when the destructions took place!

When they reached Golgotha the final, excruciatingly painful episode of punishment began:[14]

> First, the upright wood was planted in the ground. It was not high, and probably the Feet of the Sufferer were not above one or two feet from the ground. Thus could the communication described in the Gospels take place between Him and others; thus, also might His Sacred Lips be moistened with the sponge attached to the short stalk of hyssop. Next, the transverse wood . . . was placed on the ground, and the Sufferer laid on it, when His Arms were extended, drawn up, and bound to it. Then . . . a strong, sharp nail was driven, first into the Right, then into the Left Hand. . . . Next, the Sufferer was drawn up by means of ropes, perhaps ladders; the transverse either bound or nailed to the upright, and a rest or support for the Body . . . fastened on it. Lastly, the Feet were extended, and either one nail hammered into each, or a large piece of iron through the two. . . . And so might the crucified hang for hours, even days, in the unutterable anguish of suffering, till consciousness at last failed.[15]

After nailing the condemned to the crossbar and affixing that bar to the upright, it was customary to also tie or rope his arms and legs to the cross for added support; however, there is no scriptural evidence on whether this was done to Christ. We do know that just prior to the Lord being cruelly nailed upon the cross, his outer garments and his sandals were removed from his body and divided between the four soldiers who attended him. Then his inner garment or cloak was removed, but it was of such fine quality (woven without seam) that the soldiers cast lots for it rather than destroy it — thus fulfilling one of the Old Testament prophesies concerning the Savior's death (Psalm 22:18).

Vinegar or wine was offered to the Savior prior to his cross being raised to an upright position. The custom was a Jewish one, perhaps initiated to placate their traditions concerning the suffering of the body.[16] The wine contained gall or myrrh, which was an opiate[17] given to relieve some of the physical pain. Jesus tasted it, recognized what it contained, and refused to drink, apparently so that his faculties would not be dulled. The sign identifying his charges was then fastened on the cross above his head. These signs (or "titles") normally hung around the condemned prisoners' necks as they carried their crosses through the streets, or at times the guards carried them in advance of the prisoners. Although the Gospels make it appear that the Jewish leadership complained of Christ's sign after it had been placed upon his cross, it is unlikely that they would have waited until then to say something about it. In all probability they learned of the epitaph before Jesus began carrying his cross through Jerusalem, and probably complained to Pilate at the time.[18] The title read JESUS OF NAZARETH THE KING OF THE JEWS and was written in Hebrew, Greek, and Latin. The Jewish leadership wanted it to state that Jesus *claimed* to be the king of the Jews, for they feared that the title might influence some of the visitors at the feast. Pilate, who had perhaps devised the sign in an effort to antagonize these rulers who had precipitated the crucifixion, refused to change the sign, stating, "What I have written, I have written."

After the Lord's cross had been thrust upright, he uttered the words, "Father, forgive them; for they know not what they do" (Luke 23:34). This was not a forgiveness for all those involved in his crucifixion; rather, it related solely to the soldiers, who were carrying out their orders in completing the crucifixion (JST, Luke 23:35).[19] Even in his agony, the Savior granted mercy to the unwitting instruments of their Lord's death.

Death by crucifixion is slow. While Christ hung in agony hour after hour, the soldiers taunted him and mocked him with toasts of wine while they waited for him to die — not because they believed or disbelieved in him as the Son of God but because he represented the conquered Jews whom they despised.[20] They were joined in

their vile mockery by the same Jewish leaders who had contrived
and confirmed the Savior's death. Ironically, their taunts sum-
marized Christ's mission in life: "Ah, thou that destroyest the
temple, and buildest it in three days," they mocked (yet it was
Jesus who had taught them the relationship between Israel, the
temple, and their God). "He saved others; let him save himself, if
he be Christ, the chosen of God," they said (yet only through
Christ could eternal salvation be obtained). "If thou be the Son of
God," they jeered (as Satan had done when he challenged Jesus in
the wilderness. Matthew 4:3). Finally, "If he be the King of Israel,
let him now come down from the cross, and we will believe him"
(as if by some mighty miracle their evil could miraculously be
changed to good). But Christ knew that they would not repent
"though one rose from the dead" (Luke 16:31). The authors of the
Gospels related these mocking comments with different emphasis:
Matthew and Mark emphasized the Jews' doubt and their use of
blasphemy; Luke described the reasons for their mockery; and
John reads like an eyewitness account of their actions.[21]

While the Savior was fasting in the wilderness, the devil had
challenged his Messiahship, cunningly disguising his temptations
in an attempt to create doubt in the Savior's mind regarding his
trust in the Father. Now, influenced by that same king of evil, both
the heathen Romans and the Jewish leaders would again challenge
that trust. Nevertheless, their jeers, which were intended to make
Christ think that God had forsaken him, went unheeded and he
gave them no response.

Two thieves had been sentenced to be crucified with Jesus, perhaps to emphasize the power of Rome over their hostile Jewish
subjects and to strike terror into the crowd attending the Passover
feast.[22] Both thieves had initially participated with the multitude in
mocking the Savior, but eventually one of them had second
thoughts, and, perhaps moved by the Spirit, spoke of the Savior's
innocence. Without knowing whether Christ was the Messiah, he
requested the Lord's intercession in His kingdom. The request elicited Christ's second comment during his crucifixion: "Verily I say
unto thee, To day shalt thou be with me in paradise" (Luke
23:43)[23]—not that the thief would reside in the Father's celestial
kingdom, but that immediately after his death he would in general

terms be in the same place in which the Savior would be: "in the world of spirits."

John's detailed account of the crucifixion stops at this point, and resumes after the Savior has been on the cross for about two hours. It would appear that due to the haste with which the Savior had been tried and taken to be crucified, many of his immediate loved ones and close disciples had not been told what was happening. Undoubtedly John had followed the procession from Pilate's judgment hall to Golgotha and, after witnessing the Savior being affixed to the cross, had gone to alert the Lord's family and some of the disciples. He soon returned with Mary, the mother of Jesus; her sister; Mary, the wife of Clopas; and Mary Magdalene — all of whom his gospel records as being present at the crucifixion. How long they remained there is unknown.[24]

When the Savior looked down and saw his mother near the cross, he uttered his third statement: "Woman, behold thy son! Then saith he to the disciple [John], Behold thy mother!" (John 19:26-27.) The statement implied that John would now be responsible for Mary's care, and he immediately took her to his home, away from the pain and sorrow of the crucifixion. Again John's account lacks detail until he returns.[25] While John was away, the remaining women (and other disciples that had gathered) moved away from the cross and watched the remainder of the crucifixion proceedings from a distance. The Lord had almost completed his earthly mission, yet while he hung from the cross he prayed for those who had ignorantly paticipated in his death, gave comfort to the penitent, and provided for those closest to him.

It was the "sixth hour," or about noon, and Jesus had been suffering for about three hours: the records testify that the sun darkened, and it remained dark and ominous until the "ninth hour."[26] The source of the darkness is not explained and there is no historical evidence of an eclipse; however, the darkness dramatized the depths to which men had sunk, a divine manifestation of the gloom which shrouded the earth over the death of its creator.[27] The long, three-hour period of agony that the Lord experienced while he hung upon the cross in darkness concluded the atonement he had begun in the Garden of Gethsemane. He was now giving his life for all mankind, literally dying for the sins of the world: the King of kings was fulfilling his mission and was not unworthy of his kingdom, but the Jewish "kingdom," by its very words and deeds, was unworthy of its King.

The end was near by the time the Lord uttered his fourth declaration from the cross, crying in a loud voice, "My God, my God, why hast thou forsaken me?" (Matthew 27:46.) It was the climax of his suffering, for the Father had to withdraw to allow the Son to complete his mission.[28] How fitting it is that even in this he was misunderstood: the Jews thought that he had cried for Elias to assist him, and again the crowd jeered.

Almost immediately the Lord uttered his fifth statement, crying, "I thirst" (John 19:28). One of the soldiers approached to give him some vinegar on a sponge fastened to the end of a hyssop, some of the "rough wine" that they had been drinking as the vigil wore on, but others in the multitude shouted to withhold the refreshment to see if Elias would, in fact, come and save him. Ignoring the crowd, the soldier offered the vinegar to the Savior; he accepted it, fulfilling the prophecy given by the Psalmist centuries before: "They gave me also gall for my meat; and in my thirst they gave me vinegar to drink" (Psalm 69:21).

By now the Savior had been on the cross for more than six hours. He had endured all things and had faithfully completed his mission. In recognition of his victory won, he uttered his sixth comment, proclaiming: "It is finished" (John 19:30).

The seventh comment—and the final words of the dying Savior—came quickly: "Father," he announced, "into thy hands I commend my spirit" (Luke 23:46). The Lord of Hosts was dead! One of the Roman guards, apparently impressed by the Savior's demeanor throughout his torture and crucifixion, commented, "Truly this was the Son of God."

With the end of the Messiah's mortal life the veil of the temple, which shrouded the holy of holies from the holy place, was rent in twain from top to bottom, exposing the holy of holies. The veil was an enormous structure: it has been reported that to manipulate it required three hundred priests.[29] It was sixty feet high and thirty feet wide, approximately as thick as the palm of a hand, and made of seventy-two separate squares sewn together. Only once a year was the officiating priest allowed to part the veil and enter the holy of holies — the place where God dwelt, where he had shown himself to the children of Israel, and (although now empty) where the tokens of his goodness to them had been kept for many years.[30] God's hand had rent the veil as a sign to the chosen people that he had deserted both them and the temple.[31] A great earthquake shook the ground and the rocks were rent as the earth itself mourned the loss of its God.

Evening was approaching, and Jewish law required that the bodies of the condemned not be left hanging upon the cross overnight (Deuteronomy 21:22–23). Crucifixion was a dilatory method of death that "lasted not only for hours but days;"[32] however, without thought for the ignoble death of the Savior, the chief priests petitioned Pilate to shorten the suffering of the two thieves so that their execution could be completed before the Sabbath began.

As the Passover (or the first Paschal day) ended, the Sabbath began: this particular Sabbath was also considered a "high day" because it was the "second Paschal Day, which was regarded as in every respect equally sacred with the first" day, or the Passover itself.[33] Roman law required that malefactors remain on the cross for several days after their deaths, but the Romans had granted the Jews an exception to this requirement[34] so that their Sabbath would not be violated. The extreme cruelty of the Roman conquerors was sharply manifest when the soldiers took large clubs or hammers and struck the knees of the two thieves, breaking their legs before they completed the execution by running them through with a lance. When they came to Jesus they found that he had already died; therefore, again in fulfillment of prophesy (Psalm 34:20; see also Exodus 12:46; Numbers 9:12), the Lord's bones were not broken. To make sure he was dead, however, the soldiers pierced his side with a lance (Zechariah 12:10; 13:6), completing the Old Testament prophecies concerning his death. John's narrative is very specific, indicating that both blood and water gushed forth from the Savior's open wound; further, he bore testimony that he personally witnessed the event. John later used the symbolism of blood and water to teach that salvation comes through Christ's atonement and that we are born again through him: born of the water through baptism, born of the Spirit by his confirming witness, and then cleansed of our sins by the blood of Christ (1 John 5:1–8).

The Sabbath was rapidly approaching as the Savior died, so a wealthy member of the Sanhedrin, Joseph of Arimathaea (who had not consented to the proceedings but was secretly a disciple of the Savior), went to Pilate to ask for Jesus' body. Pilate was surprised that the Savior had died so quickly and questioned the soldiers to confirm the death. After he was sure the Savior was dead, he agreed to give the body to Joseph. The body was quickly wrapped in a linen cloth and taken to Joseph's tomb, which had recently been hewn out of the rock and in which no body had ever rested. The entrance to the tomb opened into a nine-foot square court area, where a bier had been placed for the body to rest on.[35] At this point Nicodemus (another member of the Sanhedrin) appeared, carrying ointment to help prepare the body for burial. The linen cloth that Christ had been carefully wrapped in at Golgotha was now taken from his body and stripped into pieces. With the application of the ointments, each of the Savior's limbs and the body were wrapped in the Jewish manner of burial.[36] No other disciples assisted, but several women stood outside the tomb and watched as their Master was laid to rest. After the body had been hastily prepared, the two Sanhedrists left the tomb and rolled a large stone over its entrance.

Even though the Sabbath had commenced, the Savior's avowed enemies were not content with his death and burial. Remembering that Jesus had prophesied he would rise again the third day, they went to Pilate and requested that the tomb be sealed and guarded, using the excuse that some of his disciples might come and steal the body, then falsely claim that the Resurrection had taken place. They were granted the watch and, even though night had fallen, they apparently returned to the tomb to seal the stone covering the entrance, thus violating their Law and defiling their Sabbath.

Jesus Christ's death sealed the fate of all those who had precipitated it. For thirty pieces of silver, Judas had bartered away the crown and the throne the Savior had promised him. The Jewish leadership were relieved of a bitter enemy when Christ was crucified, but in the process they ensured the destruction of their temple, their city, their place, and their nation. The Roman conquerors had unwittingly participated in this tragedy and in ignorance had fulfilled the prophecies of the ancients concerning Christ's death.

The Satanic influence that had been so pervasively evident throughout Christ's arrest, trial, and crucifixion had only served to further doom its author. The victory Lucifer had temporarily won with Adam he had forever lost in Christ, for the culmination of the Savior's mortal ministry had taken place and he had won the victory over death. In accordance with the plan of salvation and with approval from a loving Father, Jesus the Messiah was dead.

In the World of Spirits

John 5:25–29

25. Verily, verily, I say unto you, The hour is coming, and now is, when the dead shall hear the voice of the Son of God: and they that hear shall live.

26. For as the Father hath life in himself; so hath he given to the Son to have life in himself;

27. And hath given him authority to execute judgment also, because he is the Son of man.

28. Marvel not at this: for the hour is coming, in the which all that are in the graves shall hear his voice,

29. And shall come forth; they that have done good, unto the resurrection of life; and they that have done evil, unto the resurrection of damnation.

D&C 138:12, 18–20, 27–37

12. And there were gathered together in one place an innumerable company of the spirits of the just, who had been faithful in the testimony of Jesus while they lived in mortality;

18. While this vast multitude waited and conversed, rejoicing in the hour of their

deliverance from the chains of death, the Son of God appeared, declaring liberty to the captives who had been faithful;

19. And there he preached to them the everlasting gospel, the doctrine of the resurrection and the redemption of mankind from the fall, and from individual sins on conditions of repentance.

20. But unto the wicked he did not go, and among the ungodly and the unrepentant who had defiled themselves while in the flesh, his voice was not raised;

27. But his ministry among those who were dead was limited to the brief time intervening between the crucifixion and his resurrection;

28. And I wondered at the words of Peter—wherein he said that the Son of God preached unto the spirits in prison, who sometime were disobedient, when once the long-suffering of God waited in the days of Noah—and how it was possible for him to preach to those spirits and perform the necessary labor among them in so short a time.

29. And as I wondered, my eyes were opened, and my understanding quickened, and

I perceived that the Lord went not in person among the wicked and the disobedient who had rejected the truth, to teach them;

30. But behold, from among the righteous, he organized his forces and appointed messengers, clothed with power and authority, and commissioned them to go forth and carry the light of the gospel to them that were in darkness, even to all the spirits of men; and thus was the gospel preached to the dead.

31. And the chosen messengers went forth to declare the acceptable day of the Lord and proclaim liberty to the captives who were bound, even unto all who would repent of their sins and receive the gospel.

32. Thus was the gospel preached to those who had died in their sins, without a knowledge of the truth, or in transgression, having rejected the prophets.

33. These were taught faith in God, repentance from sin, vicarious baptism for the remission of sins, the gift of the Holy Ghost by the laying on of hands,

34. And all other principles of the gospel that were

necessary for them to know in order to qualify themselves that they might be judged according to men in the flesh, but live according to God in the spirit.

35. And so it was made known among the dead, both small and great, the unrighteous as well as the faithful, that redemption had been wrought through the sacrifice of the Son of God upon the cross.

36. Thus was it made known that our Redeemer spent his time during his sojourn in the world of spirits, instructing and preparing the faithful spirits of the prophets who had testified of him in the flesh;

37. That they might carry the message of redemption unto all the dead, unto whom he could not go personally, because of their rebellion and transgression, that they through the ministration of his servants might also hear his words.

Cross-references

Isaiah 42:7; 61:1   1 Peter 3:18–20; 4:5–6
I Corinthians 15:29

Christ's spirit passed out of his body and into the world of spirits at his death. All men who had died prior to Christ's death (both righteous and unrighteous) were currently residing in a place known as the spirit world, and now that his mortal ministry upon the earth had ended, his ministry to those already in the spirit world commenced.

That Jesus was aware of his future mission to the spirit world is evidenced by a discussion which took place early in his mission with the rulers of the Jews just after the healing of the impotent man by the pool of Bethesda. He first declared to them his relationship with the Father, then he informed them that the hour would come "when the dead shall hear the voice of the Son of God. . . . For. . . . all that are in the graves shall hear his voice."[37]

His mission in the spirit world was twofold: (1) To proclaim the glad tidings of the resurrection, which ensured redemption from the bondage of death. (2) To establish his ministry to the dead and thus provide them with the opportunity of salvation from the effects of individual sin.[38]

There are two main divisions in the spirit world. The first is called *paradise:* this is where the righteous and repentant in mortality reside between their physical death and resurrection. The second division is generally known as *spirit prison:* this is reserved for the wicked, those who were without knowledge of the plan of salvation, and those who refused repentance when it was offered to them while in mortality.[39]

The inhabitants of paradise eagerly awaited their Lord's entry into the spirit world for it signaled his victory over death. President Joseph F. Smith saw in vision the multitude of spirits who awaited the Savior's arrival and rejoiced at being in his presence.

Isaiah foresaw the Savior's mission to the inhabitants of the spirit prison and testified that he would "bring out the prisoners from the prison . . . to proclaim liberty to the captives, and the opening of the prison to them that are bound." Peter was also aware of this ministry, and he declared that Jesus (by the spirit) "went and preached unto the spirits in prison; which sometime were disobedient, when once the longsuffering of God awaited in the days of Noah."

Those in the spirit prison had to receive the gospel so that they "might be judged according to men in the flesh, but live according to God in the spirit." Those who heard the gospel of salvation in the spirit could then reject or accept the saving ordinances vicariously performed for them by others in mortality. To accept the ordinances they must develop faith in the Lord Jesus Christ, accept his atonement and sacrifice, repent of their transgressions, and obey God's word.[40] This doctrine of vicarious ordinances, while not explicitly taught in the New Testament, was obliquely referred to by Paul, who, while arguing for the reality of the resurrection, cited the early Church's practice of baptizing living Saints for the dead. "Else what shall they do which are baptized for the dead," Paul questioned, "if the dead rise not at all? why are they then baptized for the dead?"

The righteous in the spirit world were anxious to see the Savior because they had looked upon the absence from their bodies as a bondage, and they rejoiced at the opportunity for freedom. The Lord preached liberty to these spirits by declaring the everlasting gospel, which included the doctrines of the Atonement and the Resurrection. This provided them with redemption from the fall of Adam and forgiveness from individual sin on condition of repentance. However, Christ did not personally go to the wicked, for they could not abide his presence. Yet these also would be offered salvation, through missionary work.

While in the spirit the Lord organized messengers "from among the righteous" who would use his commission and authority to preach the gospel "to the captives who were bound, even unto all who would repent of their sins and receive the gospel." These spirits fell into two categories: the first consisted of those who had died in their sins without a knowledge of the truth; the second was made of those who not only had died in their sins but also had rejected the truth while in mortality. Both groups would now be taught the saving principles of the gospel: repentance from sin, faith in the Lord, vicarious baptism for the remission of sin, and the gift of the Holy Ghost by the vicarious laying on of hands; as well as any and all other principles of the gospel necessary to qualify them to be "judged according to men in the flesh, but live according to God in the spirit."

Just as the mission of Jesus Christ extended past mortality and into the spirit world, it is reasonable to assume that *all* those who labor in his ministry while in mortality will be prepared to carry the message of redemption, after leaving mortality themselves, to those who reside in spirit prison.[41]

In addition to establishing a missionary program in the spirit world, the Lord (while yet in the spirit) raised his voice to the other sheep he had spoken of in his good shepherd discourse.[42] At his death, a mist of darkness had shrouded the Western Hemisphere as a sign to the people that he had finished his mission on earth. Now the Savior spoke to those people out of that darkness, to prepare them for his coming in a resurrected form (3 Nephi 9:15).[43]

Jesus Christ's mortal ministry lasted three years. His ministry to the spirit world lasted only three days, yet it is evident that his accomplishments in the world of spirits were far reaching. During this short period of time he made salvation available to all, as provided in God's plan.[44]

"He Is Risen"

The Resurrection

John 20:1–31

1. The first day of the week cometh Mary Magdalene early, when it was yet dark, unto the sepulchre, and seeth the stone taken away from the sepulchre.

2. Then she runneth, and cometh to Simon Peter, and to the other disciple, whom Jesus loved, and saith unto them, They have taken away the Lord out of the sepulchre, and we know not where they have laid him.

3. Peter therefore went forth, and that other disciple, and came to the sepulchre.

4. So they ran both together: and the other disciple did outrun Peter, and came first to the sepulchre.

5. And he stooping down, and looking in, saw the linen clothes lying; yet went he not in.

6. Then cometh Simon Peter following him, and went into the sepulchre, and seeth the linen clothes lie,

7. And the napkin, that was about his head, not lying with the linen clothes, but wrapped together in a place by itself.

8. Then went in also that other disciple, which came first to the sepulchre, and he saw, and believed.

9. For as yet they knew not the scripture, that he must rise again from the dead.

10. Then the disciples went away again unto their own home.

11. But Mary stood without at the sepulchre weeping: and as she wept, she stooped down, and looked into the sepulchre,

12. And seeth two angels in white sitting, the one at the head, and the other at the feet, where the body of Jesus had lain.

13. And they say unto her, Woman, why weepest thou? She saith unto them, Because they have taken away my Lord, and I know not where they have laid him.

14. And when she had thus said, she turned herself back, and saw Jesus standing, and knew not that it was Jesus.

15. Jesus saith unto her, Woman, why weepest thou? whom seekest thou? She, supposing him to be the gardener, saith unto him, Sir, if thou have borne him hence, tell me where thou hast laid him, and I will take him away.

16. Jesus saith unto her, Mary. She turned herself, and saith unto him, Rabboni; which is to say, Master.

17. Jesus saith unto her, Touch me not; for I am not yet ascended to my Father: but go to my brethren, and say unto them, I ascend unto my Father, and your Father; and to my God, and your God.

18. Mary Magdalene came and told the disciples that she had seen the Lord, and that he had spoken these things unto her.

19. Then the same day at evening, being the first day of the week, when the doors were shut where the disciples were assembled for fear of the Jews, came Jesus and stood in the midst, and saith unto them, Peace be unto you.

20. And when he had so said, he shewed unto them his hands and his side. Then were the disciples glad, when they saw the Lord.

21. Then said Jesus to them again, Peace be unto you: as my Father hath sent me, even so send I you.

22. And when he had said this, he breathed on them, and saith unto them, Receive ye the Holy Ghost:

23. Whose soever sins ye remit, they are remitted unto

them; and whose soever sins ye retain, they are retained.

24. But Thomas, one of the twelve, called Didymus, was not with them when Jesus came.

25. The other disciples therefore said unto him, We have seen the Lord. But he said unto them, Except I shall see in his hands the print of the nails, and put my finger into the print of the nails, and thrust my hand into his side, I will not believe.

26. And after eight days again his disciples were within, and Thomas with them: then came Jesus, the doors being shut, and stood in the midst, and said, Peace be unto you.

27. Then saith he to Thomas, Reach hither thy finger, and behold my hands; and reach hither thy hand, and thrust it into my side: and be not faithless, but believing.

28. And Thomas answered and said unto him, My Lord and my God.

29. Jesus saith unto him, Thomas, because thou hast seen me, thou hast believed: blessed are they that have not seen, and yet have believed.

30. And many other signs truly did Jesus in the presence of his disciples, which are not written in this book:

31. But these are written, that ye might believe that Jesus is the Christ, the Son of God; and that believing ye might have life through his name.

John 21:1—25

1. After these things Jesus shewed himself again to the disciples at the sea of Tiberias; and on this wise shewed he himself.

2. There were together Simon Peter, and Thomas called Didymus, and Nathanael of Cana in Galilee, and the sons of Zebedee, and two other of his disciples.

3. Simon Peter saith unto them, I go a fishing. They say unto him, We also go with thee. They went forth, and entered into a ship immediately; and that night they caught nothing.

4. But when the morning was now come, Jesus stood on the shore: but the disciples knew not that it was Jesus.

5. Then Jesus saith unto them, Children, have ye any meat? They answered him, No.

6. And he said unto them, Cast the net on the right side of the ship, and ye shall find. They cast therefore, and now they were not able to draw it for the multitude of fishes.

7. Therefore that disciple whom Jesus loved saith unto Peter, It is the Lord. Now when Simon Peter heard that it was the Lord, he girt his fisher's coat unto him, (for he was naked,) and did cast himself into the sea.

8. And the other disciples came in a little ship; (for they were not far from land, but as it were two hundred cubits,) dragging the net with fishes.

9. As soon then as they were come to land, they saw a fire of coals there, and fish laid thereon, and bread.

10. Jesus saith unto them, Bring of the fish which ye have now caught.

11. Simon Peter went up, and drew the net to land full of great fishes, an hundred and fifty and three: and for all there were so many, yet was not the net broken.

12. Jesus saith unto them, Come and dine. And none of the disciples durst ask him, Who art thou? knowing that it was the Lord.

13. Jesus then cometh, and taketh bread, and giveth them, and fish likewise.

14. This is now the third time that Jesus shewed himself to his disciples, after that he was risen from the dead.

15. So when they had dined, Jesus saith to Simon Peter, Simon, son of Jonas, lovest thou me more than these? He saith unto him, Yea, Lord; thou knowest that I love thee. He saith unto him, Feed my lambs.

16. He saith to him again the second time, Simon, son of Jonas, lovest thou me? He saith unto him, Yea, Lord; thou knowest that I love thee. He saith unto him, Feed my sheep.

17. He saith unto him the third time, Simon, son of Jonas, lovest thou me? Peter was grieved because he said unto him the third time, Lovest thou me? And he said unto him, Lord, thou knowest all things; thou knowest that I love thee. Jesus saith unto him, Feed my sheep.

18. Verily, verily, I say unto thee, When thou wast young, thou girdest thyself, and walkedst whither thou wouldest: but when thou shalt be old, thou shalt stretch forth thy hands, and another

shall gird thee, and carry thee whither thou wouldest not.

19. This spake he, signifying by what death he should glorify God. And when he had spoken this, he saith unto him, Follow me.

20. Then Peter, turning about, seeth the disciple whom Jesus loved following; which also leaned on his breast at supper, and said, Lord, which is he that betrayeth thee?

21. Peter seeing him saith to Jesus, Lord, and what shall this man do?

22. Jesus saith unto him, If I will that he tarry till I come, what is that to thee? follow thou me.

23. Then went this saying abroad among the brethren, that that disciple should not die: yet Jesus said not unto him, He shall not die; but, If I will that he tarry till I come, what is that to thee?

24. This is the disciple which testifieth of these things, and wrote these things: and we know that his testimony is true.

25. And there are also many other things which Jesus did, the which, if they should be written every one, I suppose that even the world itself could not contain the books that should be written. Amen.

Cross-references

Matthew 28   Mark 16   Luke 24
1 Corinthians 15:4–8   Acts 1:1–12; 17:32

John's account of the Crucifixion and the Resurrection is enhanced by the fact that he was an eyewitness, while the Synoptics seem to merely supplement his narrative.[1] All the Gospel writers tend to condense their histories of those events, but the Synoptics do so more than John—perhaps due to their lack of information. The Gospel writers were not concerned about creating an exact history of the period between the first Easter morning and the ascension some forty days later; they were concerned, however, about furnishing exact evidence of the Resurrection itself.

Matthew describes the impressions of both the Lord's enemies and his disciples on the morning of the Resurrection. He also describes the Lord's appearance on the shores of Galilee (where the miracle of the second draught of fish occurred)[2] and on the mount (where Jesus again commissioned the Apostles). Mark's record is extremely brief, summarizing the events from the viewpoint of the immediate family. Luke, the historian, details the facts of the resurrection day, but then jumps immediately to the Ascension. John, though not in close detail, describes episodes that occurred during the entire forty-day period, both in Jerusalem and in Galilee, and testifies that Jesus is the Christ, the Son of God.[3]

It is difficult to determine exactly what went through the minds of the Lord's disciples and Apostles after his death and burial, but certain scriptural evidences indicate that although they knew he was dead, they did not expect him to rise again. For example:

1. Nicodemus, one of the two Sanhedrists who saw to Jesus' burial, brought burial spices to prepare the Lord's body.
2. Some women who were disciples of Christ prepared and laid up spices during the Sabbath with the intent of returning to the tomb to properly prepare the Lord's body for burial. This suggests that they did not think the Lord's mortal body would rise from corruption to incorruption.
3. When the women saw the empty tomb, they supposed that the body of Jesus had been taken away by his enemies.
4. Although the Apostles had been told several times by the Savior that he would rise again, they disbelieved the first testimonies of the women, thinking them "as idle tales." John wrote that "as yet they knew not the scripture, that he must rise again from the dead."

In contrast to these doubts by the Lord's followers, the scriptures report that his avowed enemies, the Sanhedrists, seemed to understand some of the potential of the Lord's predictions about his resurrection (whether or not they believed in the doctrine of the resurrection), so they took precautions against the body being stolen so that they could avoid the claim of resurrection by his disciples.

Many Jews believed in the earthly kingdom that their anticipated Messiah would establish at his coming but did not believe in the resurrection. Their expectation was not that the Messiah would come as a glorified, resurrected being but that he would come in great power (as he will for his second coming) and thus establish his eternal kingdom upon the earth.[4]

The religious zealots at the time were among Christ's worst enemies, for they carried the letter of the Law out to its bitter end. They perceived Jesus as being in mortal conflict with their Law because he taught the spirit of the law rather than the letter. The zealots were triumphant after the Lord's crucifixion, for the apparent uncertainty of the disciples and the Apostles alike indicated that "nothing could have seemed more abjectly weak, more pitifully hopeless, more absolutely doomed to scorn, and extinction, and despair, than the Church which He had founded."[5] The eleven Apostles and the disciples in general were overwhelmed by the events that had taken place, and it is obvious that they did not have a clear understanding of the resurrection; yet without exception the scriptures testify that their thoughts (and even the thoughts of his enemies) were filled with and centered around Jesus Christ.

The disciples were filled with deep grief over the loss of their Master and the apparent triumph of his enemies, but this was not unexpected, for the Lord had foretold these circumstances on many occasions. In addition (especially since the Transfiguration), he had referred to his resurrection frequently.[6] But the Apostles' conception of the doctrine of resurrection was clouded because of their Jewish traditions,[7] and their understanding had not yet caught up with their devotion.

Resurrection as taught by the Lord was quite foreign to the Jewish beliefs of his day.[8] However, it appears that the Lord never intended to give his disciples a complete understanding of the resurrection during his mortal ministry. Once the Savior's resurrection had taken place, the reality of the event itself would be the best teacher and would clarify his teachings and the scriptures to their understanding. The physical evidence of the Resurrection (that is, the holes in his hands and the wound in his side) was undeniable proof that the Lord had risen from the grave, and without this evidence he may not have been believed. But given that personal experience with Christ's resurrection, they were able to truthfully testify of its reality.

Those who taught the resurrection after the fact were willing to be physically and mentally abused, tortured, and even put to death for their beliefs. A basic premise of the Apostles' instruction was resurrection from the dead. Paul emphasized this when he said to the Corinthian Saints, "And if Christ be not risen, then is our preaching vain, and your faith is also vain. Yea, and we are found false witnesses of God; . . . [and] ye are yet in your sins." (1 Corinthians 15:14–17.)

The "hands-on" experience the Apostles and disciples enjoyed provided them with a firm conviction of the Resurrection. Those who objected and disbelieved seemed to do so because resurrection required them to believe in the miraculous. It is fitting that the life of the Lord Jesus Christ closed with a miracle as great as the one with which it began. A *dead* Christ would have only been a great teacher, a wonder worker, and a prophet; but a *risen* Christ "could be the Saviour, the Life, and the Life-Giver—and as such preached to all men."[9]

Jesus died around 3:00 P.M. on Friday, and the evening sunset marked the close of the day, the *first day* in the tomb. During this time the priests in the temple (so near to Golgotha) were sacrificially offering the blood of bulls and goats for the sins of Israel, completely unconscious that blood had been shed that day in a far greater sacrifice upon the cross.

While the Lord's body lay in the tomb on Saturday, the *second day*, the last Sabbath of the old Covenant was zealously observed by the multitude of worshipers that had participated in the Feast of the Passover. During the early morning hours of Sunday, the *third day*, some who dearly loved him and mourned him were busy gathering and preparing the spices needed to properly prepare his body for burial, for their oblations performed on the day of his crucifixion had been extremely hurried so that the Sabbath could be observed.

Apparently, two groups of women were preparing to go to the tomb, perhaps planning to meet there to anoint the body. Among them were Mary Magdalene; Mary, the mother of Joses; Joanna, the wife of Chuza; Salome, the mother of James and John; and several others. Undoubtedly these were some of the same women who had participated in the vigil at Christ's crucifixion and had watched from afar as Joseph of Arithamaea and Nicodemus placed the Lord's body in the tomb and rolled a stone over its entrance. The women conversed as they traveled toward the tomb, wondering how they would remove the stone when they arrived. Apparently they were unaware that the tomb had been sealed and placed under guard, but when they reached their destination not only were the guards gone but also the stone had been rolled away.

Matthew gives an intensely interesting account of what occurred during the early morning hours on Sunday: "And, behold, there was a great earthquake: for the angel of the Lord descended from heaven, and came and rolled back the stone from the door, and sat upon it. His countenance was like lightening, and his raiment white as snow." (Matthew 28:2-3.) The seal on the stone had been broken, and the guards who had been placed to watch the tomb had been terrified by the angel and had fled to report the miraculous occurrences to the chief priests. Mary Magdalene was apparently ahead of the other women as they approached the tomb. When she saw the angel and determined that the Savior's body was no longer there, she quickly ran to inform Peter and John.

While Mary Magdalene was gone, the other women arrived at the tomb, saw that the stone had been rolled away, and entered the sepulchre. Within the sepulchre they saw an angel, "a young man sitting on the right side, clothed in a long white garment" (Mark 16:5), and they were frightened, but the heavenly messenger calmed their fears and told them that Jesus was no longer there —he had risen as he had prophesied. The angel instructed the trembling women to go to the disciples and inform them that Christ would meet them in Galilee, and they immediately left the tomb to fulfill the angel's instructions.

Meanwhile Mary Magdalene had reached Peter and John and told them of the angel and the empty tomb. The two Apostles immediately left for the sepulchre. They ran the last portion of the distance (John outran Peter), but they arrived after the other women had left. John stopped apprehensively at the entrance of the tomb, but Peter rushed past John and immediately entered. He did not see an angel, but he did observe the wrappings that had covered the Lord's body and the napkin which had covered his face. John next entered the tomb and was led to believe that the Lord had risen from the grave, "for as yet they knew not the scripture, that the Lord must rise again from the dead." Both disciples left the tomb perplexed by the Savior's disappearance and returned to their residence.

Mary Magdalene had attempted to follow Peter and John when they ran to the tomb, but she arrived after they had departed. She stood outside the sepulchre weeping, for she loved the Lord and was concerned about the fate of his sacred body. She stooped to again look into the tomb and saw two angels in white apparel, one sitting at the head and one sitting at the feet of where Christ's body had lain. Their question was simple, "Woman, why weepest thou?" Mary seemed momentarily unable to respond, but then in her grief she said, "Because they have taken away my Lord, and I know not where they have laid him."

Mary then became conscious of another presence close to her and turning, she saw a man she thought to be the gardener. This man asked, "Woman, why weepest thou? Whom seekest thou?" It was the resurrected Lord, appearing for the first time since his resurrection, but Mary, still "supposing him to be the gardener" and overwhelmed with the loss of the Lord's remains, "saith unto him, Sir, if thou have borne him hence, tell me where thou hast laid him, and I will take him away."[10]

Jesus softly spoke her name, "Mary." She immediately recognized her Savior and moved toward him, saying, "Rabboni; which is to say, Master." But the close familiarity of former days was no longer possible, and the Savior declared: "Touch me not; for I am not yet ascended to my Father. But go to my brethren, and say unto them, I ascend unto my Father, and your Father; and to my God, and your God." She immediately left to give his sacred message to the Apostles.

The other women arrived after Mary had left the tomb and also saw the angels. They, too, received instructions to tell the disciples all they had seen and heard. They were traveling to fulfill this commandment when the Lord appeared to them, greeting them with the familiar, "All hail." Immediately recognizing their Lord and Savior, they reverently knelt before him, held him by the feet, "and worshipped him."[11] The Lord instructed them to tell the brethren to go into Galilee, and they would see him there; however, when the Apostles heard the testimony of Mary Magdalene and the other women, they felt that their words were "idle tales," and they believed them not.

During this time, the guards who had watched Christ's tomb had gone to the chief priests to report all that had occurred. The chief priests disbelieved their report —just as they had disbelieved all of the mighty witnesses that Jesus had given them throughout his ministry —but to be safe they bribed the guards to spread the rumor that they had fallen asleep, and that while they were asleep Jesus' disciples had stolen his body so as to be able to claim that the Resurrection had taken place. Because the guards feared Pilate's punishment if he learned they had slept on their watch, the chief priests told them that they would intercede on their behalf and absolve them of any guilt.

The news of Christ's resurrection no doubt spread rapidly among his disciples, but the reality of the Resurrection seemed too difficult for them to comprehend. The disciples knew that the Savior had died, but they were slow to understand that his death was but a prelude to his resurrection; as a result, the disciples appeared to have lost all hope, and their visions of the Messiah's earthly kingdom were dashed.[12]

According to Luke, it was probably early in the afternoon on Sunday when two of the disciples left Jerusalem for Emmaus. One of the two disciples was named Cleopas; the other remains unnamed, but it is traditionally thought that it was Luke himself. As they traveled, they discussed that eventful day and were bewildered and confused by it all.[13] Somewhere along their route a stranger joined them in their travels. The scripture states that their eyes "were holden" in order that they might not recognize the Lord. He asked them about their discussion and wondered why they were sad. Cleopas asked whether he was a stranger to Jerusalem and did not know what had taken place there. He then rehearsed all that had transpired during the fateful days from Friday to Sunday morning. He explained that Jesus had been well known, even considered to be a prophet by the people, and that the chief priests had condemned him to death and crucified him. He expressed the disciples' belief concerning Jesus, "that it had been he which should have redeemed Israel," and they indicated that it had been three days since his death.

He continued, telling the "stranger" that certain women had gone to the sepulchre early that very morning and had been astonished when they could not find the Savior's body. The women had reported this to the disciples and the Apostles, testifying that they had seen a vision of angels who had announced that Jesus was alive. Evidently, Cleopas and his companion had spoken to Peter and John, for Cleopas noted that certain of the Apostles had gone to the sepulchre to verify what the women had seen and that the body was in fact gone —but Peter and John had not seen the angels.

The Savior listened quietly, then, without identifying himself, he reproved Cleopas and Luke, noting that they had been slow of heart to believe what the prophets had spoken. He began to recite evidence that Christ should have suffered all of these things in order to enter his glory, and he enumerated the scriptures as evidence, beginning with the writings of Moses and continuing through all of the prophets. As they approached Emmaus, the stranger indicated that he planned to keep traveling, but the two disciples "constrained him" (having felt of the Spirit without recognizing the Lord), and they asked him to sup with them and abide with them throughout the evening. The Lord agreed, and as dinner commenced he "took bread and blessed it, and brake and gave to them." With the performance of this familiar event their eyes were opened and they knew their Savior, but then he "vanished out of their sight."[14] At this point the disciples acknowledged how their hearts had burned within them while the "stranger" had been opening the scriptures to their understanding, and in their excitement they arose from their dinner and returned to Jerusalem that same night.

It is apparent that sometime during that same afternoon the Lord appeared to Peter, for Paul later testifies to the Corinthians of that appearance (1 Corinthians 15:5). Undoubtedly this personal witness to the senior Apostle was for his instruction and edification so that he could strengthen others in their conviction of the Resurrection.

When Cleopas and Luke reached Jerusalem, they found the Apostles and other disciples gathered together in an upper room for their evening meal. The scriptures note that they had shut both the outer and the inner doors to the house "for fear of the Jews."

They may have been apprehensive because they were Christ's disciples and still suspect, or perhaps they thought the stories of the empty tomb might have reached the authorities, who would again incite the hatred of the Sanhedrists. In any case, they took special precautions to prevent detection. By this time they knew that Christ had risen, but they still did not understand the Resurrection itself. While they were thus assembled Christ suddenly appeared to them, and they were terrified because they thought that they were seeing a "spirit" or ghost.

The Savior allayed their fears and misunderstandings by commanding them to not only look at his hands and feet but also touch him so that they would know that he was not a spirit, for spirits did not have bodies of flesh and bones as they could see he had. As if to emphasize his reality, the Lord took a piece of their broiled fish and some honeycomb and ate before them. Then, as he had with the two disciples on the road to Emmaus, he expounded the scriptures to them and opened the eyes of their understanding so they could comprehend why he had to suffer in order that he might rise again.

The Apostles were instructed to carry on the work that Christ had begun, preaching repentance and remission of sins in his name to all nations. He authorized them to do this work just as the Father had authorized him, and he gave them the Holy Ghost to sustain them in their calling. He told them that they had the power to either remit or retain sins, and in addition to this power he bestowed the keys of the priesthood upon them so that they could preserve the integrity of the Church and provide for its administrative needs. Thomas was absent when the Lord made this appearance to the Apostles, and when he was told of the marvelous occurrence he refused to believe unless he personally could witness the corporeality of the Lord.

Apparently a quiet week passed wherein the Messiah did not appear, but on the first day of the following week the Apostles again gathered in a closed room and the Savior appeared in their midst. This time Thomas was present, and when he had seen the Lord's hands and felt his side his doubts fled and he eagerly accepted the Resurrection by acknowledging his Lord and God. Jesus again taught the Apostles concerning the Resurrection, but now he led them away from the physical evidence and directed them to the higher element of faith—blessing those who believed and understood the reality of the resurrected Savior without having to see him. John concluded this account of the Savior's appearance with his personal testimony:[15] "But these [things] are written, that ye might believe that Jesus is the Christ, the Son of God; and that believing ye might have life through his name" (John 20:31).

A short time later the Apostles left Jerusalem for Galilee to await the Lord's promised visit. They undoubtedly testified to other disciples of the Resurrection; however, some doubted, even though some apparently accompanied the Apostles as they travelled to Galilee. Perhaps it was during this trip that the Lord appeared on a mountain (Matthew 28:16) to the group of "five hundred at once" that Paul mentions in Corinthians (1 Corinthians 15:6).

The brethren soon arrived in Galilee. While they were waiting for the Savior, Peter and six of the Apostles decided to go fishing. That night they fished on the lake but caught nothing. With the approach of dawn they saw a man standing on the beach. He asked them if they had caught any fish, and their response was negative. He then directed them to cast their net on the right side of the boat, and as soon as they complied their net was filled to overflowing. John then recognized the stranger and whispered to Peter that it was the Lord. Peter, eager to get to his Master, drew his fisher's coat around him and cast himself into the sea. The ship was still approximately 350 feet from shore, so the others followed in a small boat, dragging the heavy net of fish with them.[16]

The Savior had built a fire and had the morning meal ready and waiting for the Apostles. He instructed them to bring in the load of fish they had caught, and Peter returned to the shore to help his fellow Apostles pull the overburdened net onto the beach. Jesus then bade the Apostles eat the meal he had prepared, but some of them were still apprehensive. Though they knew he was the Lord they did not dare ask him to confirm it.

After they had finished dining, Jesus summoned Peter to him and asked, "Lovest thou me more than these?" Peter understood what the Lord was asking him, for the Lord had told Peter that he would deny him thrice before the cock crowed. Peter had confidently asserted that he would not deny the Lord but would follow him even to death. However, he had denied the Lord, and those

denials were "uncancelled before the other disciples, nay, before
Peter himself."[17] Peter knew that he needed the Savior's forgive-
ness, and he responded with great humility when he said, "Yea,
Lord; thou knowest that I love thee." The Lord simply responded,
"Feed my lambs."

Again the Lord looked upon Peter and said, "Lovest thou me?"
Peter responded as before, to which the Lord replied, "Feed my
sheep." A third time the Savior looked upon his chief Apostle and
said, "Lovest thou me?" Undoubtedly Peter recognized the parallel
between the Lord's three-times-asked question and his thrice-given
denial and was grieved. In anguish Peter cried, "Lord, thou
knowest all things; thou knowest that I love thee," and this time
Jesus authoritatively commanded, "Feed my sheep." Peter's repentance was accepted and the Savior forgave him. The Lord acknowledged his chief Apostle's strength and the great work which
he would do in furthering the kingdom, but he prophesied that
eventually Peter would give his life for the gospel—martyred in
the same manner that the Lord had been.

Jesus then directed his chief Apostle to "Follow me," apparently inviting Peter to move away from the other Apostles
where they could talk privately. The Lord walked away from the
group and Peter followed him, as did John, "the disciple whom
Jesus loved." Peter, noticing that John was following, inquired
with brotherly interest what the Lord expected of John. The Lord
responded that he would not die but would tarry until the Messiah
came again, a blessing which is attested to in modern revelation
(D&C 7). Although Paul mentions that the Lord also appeared to
James (1 Corinthians 15:7), this was the third and last recorded
time that the Savior appeared to the Apostles as a whole until the
Ascension. However, John testifies that the Lord did "many other
things," and that if they were written, "the world itself could not
contain the books."

The Ascension

Whether on the shores of Galilee or at Jerusalem, the Lord had
renewed the apostolic commission to all of his Apostles. Now, as
the time of Jesus' ascension approached, they gathered on the
slopes of the Mount of Olives, "which is from Jerusalem a sabbath

day's journey" (Acts 1:12). The Lord blessed his special witnesses with the promises the Father had given him and declared that with his resurrection the Father had given him "all power . . . in heaven and in earth." The Apostles again asked the Savior when the kingdom would be restored to Israel, but the question went unanswered, for the promises the Lord gave and the powers he bestowed were spiritual, not worldly (Acts 1:6–8). The Apostles were instructed to tarry in Jerusalem until they were endowed with power from heaven—the fulfillment of which came on the day of Pentecost when the Holy Ghost was manifested to them (Acts 2:2–3). When that had been accomplished (and only then), they were to go forth to all nations, teaching the commandments, witnessing Christ's resurrection, and baptizing in the name of the Father, the Son, and the Holy Ghost.

The Savior lifted up his hands and blessed them, promising that he would be with them always—then he miraculously ascended and a cloud received him out of their sight. Suddenly, two angels stood beside the Apostles and asked, "Ye men of Galilee, why stand ye gazing up into heaven? this same Jesus, which is taken up from you into heaven, shall so come in like manner as ye have seen him go into heaven."

The Apostles returned to Jerusalem "with great joy"—and no wonder! The Lord had risen—they were witnesses of it—and his work of salvation would continue both on earth and in heaven until the end of time.

Part Four

The Way,
the Truth,
and the Life

Establishing the Kingdom   *10*

Other Sheep

John 10:16

16. And other sheep I have, which are not of this fold: them also I must bring, and they shall hear my voice; and there shall be one fold, and one shepherd.

3 Nephi 15:21-24

21. And verily I say unto you, that ye are they of whom I said: Other sheep I have which are not of this fold; them also I must bring, and they shall hear my voice; and there shall be one fold, and one shepherd.

22. And they understood me not, for they supposed it had been the Gentiles; for they understood not that the Gentiles should be converted through their preaching.

23. And they understood me not that I said they shall hear my voice; and they understood me not that the Gentiles should not at any time hear my voice—that I

should not manifest myself unto them save it were by the Holy Ghost.

24. But behold, ye have both heard my voice, and seen me; and ye are my sheep, and ye are numbered among those whom the Father hath given me.

3 Nephi 16:1

1. And verily, verily, I say unto you that I have other sheep, which are not of this land, neither of the land of Jerusalem, neither in any parts of that land round about whither I have been to minister.

Cross-references

3 Nephi 1, 7, 8, 9, 10, 16–28   Helaman 14

The Book of Mormon records that six hundred years before his birth as Jesus Christ, Jehovah, the God of the Old Testament, appeared to a prophet then living in the vicinity of Jerusalem. Lehi was commanded by the Lord to take his family and leave Jerusalem for a "promised land" before that destruction prophesied by Jeremiah took place. He took his family and the family of Ishmael and travelled in the wilderness for approximately eight years. They then built a ship, crossed the oceans, and arrived on the Western Hemisphere (the "promised land") after a period of "many days." (1 Nephi 10:4; 3 Nephi 1:1.)

These people soon divided into two main groups, generally known as the Nephites and the Lamanites. Throughout the centuries prior to Christ's birth the people maintained this division, and for the most part continual animosity existed between them.

Approximately five years prior to the birth of the Savior in Jerusalem, a righteous Lamanite prophet named Samuel was sent to the Nephites (who had become more wicked than the Lamanites at this time) to call them to repentance in preparation for the advent of their Savior — but they became angry and would not listen to him. To convince his hearers that the Savior would soon be born, Samuel gave them a very specific sign. He prophesied that on the night before His birth there would be no darkness — that is, there would be a day, a night, and a day wherein no darkness would occur; and in addition, a new star would appear in the heavens. By these signs they would know that all that had been prophesied concerning the birth of the Lord was true.

During the time of Christ's mortal probation on the Eastern Hemisphere, Book of Mormon prophets on the Western Hemisphere were declaring his truths so that their people might also know of the Savior. The ministry of these prophets "mirrored" the events in Christ's ministry, in order to testify of him. The people of the Western Hemisphere knew of the people in Jerusalem, for they had come from there, but the people in Jerusalem knew nothing of their fellow tribesmen in the West.

John records two discourses the Savior delivered during his last visits to Jerusalem (John 10:1–42). They have become known as the "good shepherd discourse." The first portion of this discourse (verses 1–21) was delivered while the Savior was at the Feast of Tabernacles; two months later, while he was at the Feast of Dedication, he delivered the remaining portion (verses 22–42). The Lord declared his Messiahship in these sermons, using the allegory of the good shepherd.[1] The allegory was a familiar one in his day and was frequently used by the rabbis. In the allegory Jesus referred to the people in Jerusalem as his sheep, but he declared to them that he had *other* sheep which were not of the Jewish fold. These other sheep were also to hear his voice, for there was but one fold and one shepherd. The "other sheep" included (1) those who, under Jehovah's direction, had migrated from Jerusalem to the Western Hemisphere, and (2) the lost ten tribes of Israel (3 Nephi 21:26). The Jews did not understand the reference: they thought of the "other sheep" as the Gentiles, to whom the chosen people were obligated to provide the means of salvation. But Jesus had declared that he had been specifically sent to the house of Israel, not to the Gentiles (who would have the gospel preached to them by his Apostles after his death).

The "other sheep" of the Western Hemisphere could not receive Christ in his mortality, for that was reserved for the Jews in Palestine; however, in his place they would receive great signs and wonders that would reveal to them his birth, his ministry, and his death. But such was the prevailing wickedness that as the prophesied time of Christ's birth approached, the wicked declared a "special day" upon which they would put to death the Lord's followers if the sign did not occur.

As this designated day drew near, the prophet Nephi fervently prayed to God that he might know of the time when the sign would be given. The Lord responded by telling him that upon that very night the sign would be given, and that the next day he would be born.

When the sun fell below the horizon that evening no darkness fell upon the land, and all through the night it was as light "as though it was midday" (3 Nephi 1:19). When morning came, the sun rose again. Thus came a day, a night, and a day without darkness. Also a new star appeared in the firmament. These events confirmed the prophecy and testified to the people on the Western Hemisphere that the Son of God — "the light of the world" — had been born in the East.

The sign was significant and had not been chosen by accident. During his ministry, at a celebration known as the Feast of Tabernacles, the Savior would use those very words to declare his divinity. At this feast four giant candelabra in the temple were lighted and burned throughout the night, providing light for the courts of the temple and illuminating "every court in Jerusalem."[2] The light from the candelabra represented the light of Jehovah, and the symbolic meaning of this part of the celebration was found in the "express Messianic expectation of the Rabbis."[3]

Jesus based one of his greatest discourses on this celebration,[4] and he explained its symbolism by declaring to the rulers and to the people gathered in the temple at Jerusalem, "I am the light of the world" (John 8:12). He was *indeed* the light of the world, and while he declared it with such rich symbolism to the people in Judea he also declared it to the people on the Western Hemisphere with an even greater sign — by literally lighting the sky the night he was born — for the "light of the world" had come.

But the Western Hemisphere sheep quickly forgot the sign of Christ's birth, and as he grew into youth and early manhood in the East the people of the West again became wicked and disbelieving. As the time for Christ's ministry approached, another prophet named Nephi (the son of Nephi) was raised up. He would administer in Christ's stead to the children of Lehi.

The Book of Mormon reports that Nephi was called by angels, and that power was given to him not only to know of his Savior but also to know about the Savior's personal ministry as it was taking place in the East. He, in turn, was called to teach repentance to the people on the Western Hemisphere and to testify of the divinity of Christ. During his ministry, angels administered to him daily. As the Christ performed mighty miracles in the East, Nephi mirrored His work by performing mighty miracles in the West — casting out devils, healing the sick, and raising his brother, Timothy, from the dead. Just as the Lord was being rejected on the Eastern Hemisphere, Nephi, as a special witness for Christ, was being rejected on the Western Hemisphere. The reaction of the Jews to the Lord's miracles was one of anger and disbelief, and Nephi elicited the same response from his other sheep (3 Nephi 7).

Just as Samuel the Lamanite had prophesied of the birth of Christ, so too had he prophesied of his death, testifying of the great darkness and destruction that would come upon the Western Hemisphere at that time.

The Bible testifies that while Jesus hung upon the cross from the sixth to the ninth hour, the sun was darkened, and the earth prepared for the "light of the world" to be extinguished from mortality. In the West a similar phenomenon commenced: for the space of three hours (which correlated with the sixth to the ninth hours in Jerusalem) a storm arose, "such an one as never had been known in all the land." The tempest was enormous: "there was terrible thunder, insomuch that it did shake the whole earth as if it was about to divide asunder. And there were exceedingly sharp lightnings, such as never had been known in all the land." (3 Nephi 8:5-7.) Cities caught fire and sank into the sea, some were buried by the earth, and the whole face of the land was changed. Great whirlwinds occurred which carried people off to unknown consequences, and highways that had been travelled for hundreds of years were broken up and rocks were rent and the face of the earth was drastically changed.

At the conclusion of this three-hour period Christ gave up the ghost and died, the veil of the temple in Jerusalem was rent in twain, and the earth quaked. In the West a thick darkness came upon all the face of the land, a darkness so dense that the people could not see, no means of light could be lit, and no fire could be kindled (3 Nephi 8:22).

This intense darkness continued while the body of Jesus lay in the tomb. And the survivors mourned, wept, and lamented that as a people they had not repented of their wickedness while there was still time. Then, out of the darkness, came a voice, "Wo, wo, wo unto this people; wo unto the inhabitants of the whole earth except they shall repent; for the devil laugheth, and his angels rejoice, because of the slain of the fair sons and daughters of my people." It was the spirit of Jesus Christ speaking, and he explained that he had caused so great a destruction upon their land because of the wickedness of the people. He wanted "to hide their wickedness and abominations from before [his] face." (3 Nephi 9:2, 7.)

He declared to them, "O all ye that are spared because ye were more righteous than they, will ye not now return unto me, and repent of your sins, and be converted, that I may heal you?" (3 Nephi 9:13.) He instructed them that there should be no more sacrifices or burnt offerings, because (as the scriptures had foretold) the Law of Moses had been fulfilled in him, that they should offer instead a broken heart and a contrite spirit. When the Lord concluded his message there was silence for many hours; then his voice was heard again, calling the people to repentance and painfully reminding them that they had had the opportunity to repent many times before, but had passed it by.

Slowly the three days passed. At last, when Christ was resurrected, the darkness in the West dispersed — the light of the world had come out of the tomb. The resurrected Lord administered to his Apostles and disciples for forty days in the East. During that time the people in the West marvelled at the great destruction in their land and started to reestablish order in their lives. When his work with the Apostles on the Eastern Hemisphere was finished, the Savior ascended into heaven, whence he would soon descend again. This time to visit his other sheep on the Western Hemisphere.[5]

"And now it came to pass that there [was] a great multitude gathered together, of the people of Nephi, round the temple which was in the land Bountiful" (3 Nephi 11:1). While they were conversing they heard a voice, "as if it came out of heaven; and they cast their eyes round about, for they understood not the voice which they heard" (3 Nephi 11:3). A second time the soft voice was heard, but they still could not understand it. Finally, the third time they understood. The voice said: "Behold my Beloved Son, in whom I am well pleased, in whom I have glorified my name —hear ye him" (3 Nephi 11:7). As the people looked toward the sky they saw a Man in a white robe descending out of heaven. He declared unto them, "Behold, I am Jesus Christ, whom the prophets testified shall come into the world" (3 Nephi 11:10). The Lord had come to his "other sheep."

The Lord established the same doctrines and practices in the West as he had in the East. He instructed the people in gospel principles and informed them that the Mosaic Law was fulfilled. He taught them the ordinances of baptism, established the sacrament, and preached the Sermon on the Mount. He selected twelve disciples, gave them power in the priesthood, and charged them with the responsibility of promulgating the gospel. He resolved the contentions of the people and established the name by which his Church should be called. He declared that he still had "other sheep" whom he must visit in order to complete his mission to the covenant people (the twelve tribes of Israel), and finally he promised the twelve disciples that if they were faithful he would grant them their heart's desire. Nine of the disciples immediately stepped forward and requested that upon their deaths they be transmitted directly into the Lord's kingdom. The last three remained silent, and whether the Lord had taught them of John's request in the East or not, he knew that that was what they wanted —to be able to remain on the earth and work to bring souls unto Christ until the Lord's second coming. Their wish was granted. The Lord then ascended into heaven.

The Messiah who testified and witnessed to the chosen people on the Eastern Hemisphere also testified and witnessed to the chosen people on the Western Hemisphere. There were no differences in the teachings he presented, nor should there have been, for Christ's ministry is given for the salvation of *all* God's children. That a record of both civilizations was kept by the Lord's prophets and preserved for our use is a blessing that cannot be overstated, for in all things both the Bible and the Book of Mormon serve as witnesses for the divinity of Jesus Christ.

The Restoration:
In the Fulness of Times

Joseph Smith — History 1:10–17

10. In the midst of this war of words and tumult of opinions, I often said to myself: What is to be done? Who of all these parties are right; or, are they all wrong together? If any one of them be right, which is it, and how shall I know it?

11. While I was laboring under the extreme difficulties caused by the contests of these parties of religionists, I was one day reading the Epistle of James, first chapter and fifth verse, which reads: *If any of you lack wisdom, let him ask of God, that giveth to all men liberally, and up-braideth not; and it shall be given him.*

12. Never did any passage of scripture come with more power to the heart of man than this did at this time to mine. It seemed to enter with great force into every feeling of my heart. I reflected on it again and again, knowing that if any person needed wisdom from God, I did; for how to act I did not know, and unless I could get more wisdom than I then had, I would never know; for the teachers of religion of the different sects understood the same passages of scripture so differently as to destroy all confidence in settling the question by an appeal to the Bible.

13. At length I came to the conclusion that I must either remain in darkness and confusion, or else I must do as James directs, that is, ask of God. I at length came to the determination to "ask of God," concluding that if he gave wisdom to them that lacked wisdom, and would give liberally, and not up-braid, I might venture.

14. So, in accordance with this, my determination to ask of God, I retired to the woods to make the attempt. It was on the morning of a beautiful, clear day, early in the spring of eighteen hundred and twenty. It was the first time in my life that I had made such an attempt, for amidst all my anxieties I had never as yet made the attempt to pray vocally.

15. After I had retired to the place where I had previously designed to go, having

looked around me, and finding myself alone, I kneeled down and began to offer up the desires of my heart to God. I had scarcely done so, when immediately I was seized upon by some power which entirely overcame me, and had such an astonishing influence over me as to bind my tongue so that I could not speak. Thick darkness gathered around me, and it seemed to me for a time as if I were doomed to sudden destruction.

16. But, exerting all my powers to call upon God to deliver me out of the power of this enemy which had seized upon me, and at the very moment when I was ready to sink into despair and abandon myself to destruction —not to an imaginary ruin, but to the power of some actual being from the unseen world, who had such marvelous power as I had never before felt in any being—just at this moment of great alarm, I saw a pillar of light exactly over my head, above the brightness of the sun, which descended gradually until it fell upon me.

17. It no sooner appeared than I found myself delivered from the enemy which held me bound. When the light rested upon me I saw two Personages, whose brightness and glory defy all description, standing above me in the air. One of them spake unto me, calling me by name and said, pointing to the other—*This is My Beloved Son. Hear Him!*

Cross-references

Daniel 2   2 Thessalonians 2:1–3
Ephesians 1:9–10

Almost as fast as people were converted to the Church after the resurrection of Jesus, members began to fall away. Paul foresaw this problem and cautioned the Thessalonians saying: "Now we beseech you, brethren, by the coming of our Lord Jesus Christ, and by our gathering together unto him, that ye be not soon shaken in mind, or be troubled, neither by spirit, nor by word, nor by letter as from us, as that the day of Christ is at hand. Let no man deceive you by any means: for that day shall not come, except there come a falling away first, and that man of sin be revealed, the son of perdition." (2 Thessalonians 2:1–3.)

Paul knew that the apostasy, the falling away, would be long-lived and so complete that it would eventually require a restoration of the gospel. Peter also understood the falling away and the eventual need for a restoration. In one of his early discourses (given in the temple shortly after the ascension of Christ) he taught both followers and rulers alike, saying: "Repent ye therefore, and be converted, that your sins may be blotted out, when the times of refreshing shall come from the presence of the Lord; and he shall send Jesus Christ, which before was preached unto you: whom the heaven must receive until the times of restitution of all things, which God hath spoken by the mouth of all his holy prophets since the world began" (Acts 3:19–21).

Jesus had preached openly to the Jews, yet they had rejected and crucified him. After his forty-day ministry to the Apostles on the Eastern Hemisphere he ascended into heaven, and he would not come again to establish his kingdom upon the earth until after the times of restitution, or restoration, of all that had previously been prophesied by the holy prophets from the beginning of time. Daniel saw this in the interpretation to Nebuchadnezzar's dream, and indicated that *this* kingdom of God would be established in the latter days (Daniel 2:31–45). Paul also knew this when he explained, "having made known unto us the mystery of his will, according to his good pleasure which he hath purposed in himself: that in the dispensation of the fulness of times he might gather together in one all things in Christ, both which are in heaven, and which are on earth; even in him" (Ephesians 1:9–10).

As the Apostles were martyred one by one for the great cause they had espoused, the long night of apostasy began. The Dark Ages crept upon the earth and locked away men's minds and visions for centuries. Then Lucifer, the man of sin, was revealed. Although mankind continued to be bound with the forces of evil for centuries, during the Renaissance and the Reformation the Western world moved away from the darkness and into the light. As the Spirit of God moved upon men and upon nations, they were prepared for the dispensation of the fullness of times and the restoration of all things. America was founded, and in this cradle of liberty the Lord raised up certain men who established a Constitution based upon principles which would allow the gospel of Jesus

Christ to once more find a place in the hearts of mankind. (D&C 101:76–80.)

The door to the fullness of times was opened in the spring of 1820 to Joseph Smith, when in the fifteenth year of his life he went into a small grove of trees in upstate New York and knelt in prayer. God appeared in his majesty and attested to the divinity of his Son, and the "light of the world" once more shed forth his truths that man might be saved. The silence of centuries was broken, and "the current human conception of Deity as an incorporeal essence of something possessing neither definite shape nor tangible substance was" revealed as totally devoid of truth.[6] As the First Vision burst forth upon the Prophet Joseph, "he knew that the Father and the Son were individual Personages, each distinct from the other,"[7] and that their oneness, as it had been incomprehensibly formulated in the creeds of the Dark Ages, was actually a oneness "of perfection in purpose, plan, and action, as the scriptures declare it to be."[8] The Restoration had begun, and it will not cease until the second coming of the Lord Jesus Christ.

On 21 September 1823, three years after the vision of the Father and the Son, Joseph was again in prayer when a heavenly being (who announced himself as Moroni) stood before him in the air. Moroni disclosed to Joseph the location of a sacred book of scripture which would be *another witness for Christ*. The Book of Mormon records were eventually recovered and translated, and were finally published in 1830.

The authority to administer the gospel ordinances was next restored by those who had first held that authority when Christ was upon the earth. John the Baptist appeared and restored the Aaronic Priesthood on 15 May 1829 (D&C 13). Soon after that Peter, James, and John appeared and restored the Melchizedek Priesthood and the authority of the holy apostleship (D&C 27:12–13; 128:20). The Church of Jesus Christ of Latter-day Saints was officially organized on 6 April 1830 (D&C 20:1),[9] and the temple of the Restoration was constructed in Kirtland, Ohio, and dedicated on 27 March 1836 (D&C 109).

The authority and power of past dispensational leaders was restored shortly after the dedication of the Kirtland Temple when, one by one, great prophets of old appeared to Joseph Smith and Oliver Cowdery (D&C 110). Moses appeared to restore the keys of the gathering of Israel; the prophet Elias appeared to restore the gospel and the covenant of Abraham; and Elijah appeared to restore the sealing power so that all things could be bound on earth and in heaven. The prophesies of Joel concerning the second coming of Christ were soon to be fulfilled (Joel 2:28–31; Joseph Smith —History 1:41), and the marvelous work spoken of by Isaiah (which would be an ensign to the nations) had been established (Isaiah 5:26; 11:12; 29:13–14). Gabriel, Enoch, Adam, and many other prophets from the beginning of time to the dispensation of the fullness of times also appeared (D&C 128:21).

The priesthood having been restored, the call of Apostle was again given and the first Twelve Apostles of the last and final dispensation were called and ordained as special witnesses for the Lord Jesus Christ. The Lord's saving ordinances (all encompassed in what we call the gospel of Jesus Christ today) were once again available to all mankind so that they might be reunited with their Father in Heaven:

> And because it is the power of God that saves men, it includes both what the Lord does for us and what we must do for ourselves to be saved. On his part it is the atonement; on our part it is obedience to all that is given us of God. Thus the gospel includes every truth, every principle, every law —all that men must believe and know. Thus it includes every ordinance, every rite, every performance —all that men must do to please their Maker. Thus it includes every priesthood, every key, every power —all that men must receive to have their acts bound on earth and sealed eternally in heaven.[10]

The promises to the fathers and the reestablishment of the Savior's ministry have all been fulfilled in the Restoration.

The Second Coming of Jesus the Messiah — The Millennial Ministry

The last event in the mortal ministry of Jesus Christ was his ascension into heaven from the Eastern Hemisphere. As this took place, two angels stood by and exclaimed to the Apostles, "This same Jesus, which is taken up from you into heaven, shall so come in like manner as ye have seen him go into heaven" (Acts 1:11). From this point in time, many began looking forward to the second coming of Jesus Christ in the flesh — in power and great glory — "to execute judgment upon the earth and to inaugurate a reign of righteousness."[11]

Although the righteous eagerly look forward to the Lord's second coming and the ushering in of his millennial reign, the exact time of that event has never been disclosed; but the certainty of his coming is without question. It was foreseen by many Old Testament prophets, and it was looked forward to and prophesied of by prophets of both the New Testament and the latter days.[12] Although the Lord has not given the exact date of his coming, he has given certain signs that, if recognized, will alert the righteous to this great event.

The fulfillment of prophecy concerning the Second Coming commenced in 1820 with Joseph Smith's vision of God the Eternal Father and his Son Jesus Christ. The sequence of visions which followed culminated in the restoration of the gospel and the opening of the dispensation of the fullness of times.

The Jews rejected the Messiah, and because of the universal apostasy which followed that rejection and the death of the Apostles, the children of Israel (the seed of Abraham, who had been chosen to spread the gospel of salvation to all the earth) were scattered throughout the earth. One of the great signs of the Second Coming is the gathering of those lost and scattered children.

The responsibility for gathering the righteous from the world falls to the tribe of Ephraim (as the presiding tribe in Israel).[13] The descendants of Ephraim trace their lineage through Joseph, one of the original twelve tribes. Ephraim's call is similar to that of the Twelve Apostles, who, at the end of Christ's mortal ministry, were commissioned to take the gospel to all of the world. With the restoration of the gospel and the establishment of the Church, it is now Ephraim's responsibility to disseminate the gospel's saving ordinances throughout the world so that all may have the opportunity to receive these ordinances and be admitted into the Father's kingdom. This is the general gathering of the righteous from among the Gentiles and from those lost and scattered descendants of Israel (Isaiah 11:11; 43:3–12; Hosea 1:10–11; 3 Nephi 21).

"Ephraim shall assemble in Zion on the Western continent, and Judah shall be again established in the east; and the cities of Zion and Jerusalem shall be the capitals of the world empire, over which the Messiah shall reign in undisputed authority."[14]

One of the visits made by the Savior during his preparation for the Second Coming will be to his people of Judah, one of the original Twelve Tribes of Israel. The Mount of Olives shall "cleave in twain" (D&C 45:48), and there he will gather the tribe of Judah and testify and witness to them, in a manner indisputable, that he is their long-awaited Messiah (Zechariah 12:10; 13:1-6; D&C 45:51-52).

Finally, to complete the gathering, "the Lost [ten] Tribes shall be brought forth from the place where God has hidden them through the centuries and receive their long-deferred blessings at the hands of Ephraim."[15] (The return of the ten tribes will probably not take place until after the Lord's second coming — (D&C 133:25-35; Isaiah 35:8-10.)[16]

Another general sign of the Second Coming is the great wickedness which shall be upon the face of the earth prior to the Lord's advent. Indeed, the conditions of the latter-days will be comparable to the days of Noah, when evil was so powerful that God destroyed all but eight souls.[17] To cleanse the earth of this wickedness in preparation for the millennial ministry of the Savior, great destructions will come upon its inhabitants so that the more wicked (those who cannot abide his coming) will be destroyed.

Before his coming, hail and fire will rain upon the earth (Ezekiel 38:22; Revelation 8:7), the sea will be smitten and the earth's waters polluted (Revelation 8:10-11; 11:4), the plagues that John the Revelator saw will be sent forth upon the earth, and man will be tormented with noisome and grievous sores (Revelation 16:2). The sea will become like the "blood of a dead man," and "every living soul [will die] in the sea" (Revelation 16:3). The sun will also be affected so that it "[scorches] men with fire" and with great heat (Revelation 16:8), and a great darkness will occur that overcomes the minds of mankind because of their wicked ways (Revelation 16:10).[18]

Rivers will dry up and false prophets will come forth working the works of Satan, performing miracles so that they can deceive their fellowman (Revelation 16:12-14).[19] Eventually, two great prophets will be raised up to preach in Jerusalem of the coming Messiah, and their ministry will occur while the devil makes war against the city with his great army (see also Revelation 9:16). The power of these prophets will be like that of Elijah and Nephi of old, and for three and one-half years they will preach with a warning voice and cry repentance unto Judah. Finally, the armies of evil shall overcome the holy city and kill the two prophets. Their bodies will be left in the streets for three and one-half days, after which they will be caught up and received by the Messiah as he descends from heaven to appear to the tribe of Judah (Revelation 11).

While all of these calamities culminate, general conditions throughout the world will become chaotic—and a third general sign of the Lord's coming will take place. Turbulence and affliction will be the norm, and a way of life contrary to that decreed by God will be pervasive throughout the children of men. Great signs and wonders will occur: fire and vapors of smoke will appear (Joel 2:30–31); a great hailstorm will destroy the crops of the earth (D&C 29:16); flies will take hold of the earth's inhabitants (D&C 29:18); the beasts and fowls will eat men's flesh (D&C 29:20); the sun will be darkened and the moon will appear as blood (D&C 29:14; Isaiah 13:9–11); the stars will fall from heaven (D&C 29:14; 88:87); and the rainbow will cease to appear.[20] A mighty earthquake (above all earthquakes) shall shake the earth, and the land that was split in the days of Noah and Peleg (Genesis 10:25) will be reunited in paradisiacal glory (Revelation 16:18–20; D&C 133:24). As the devastations cease, a great conference will take place at Adam-ondi-Ahman[21] in preparation for the Savior's immediate coming.

Finally, the sign of the Son of Man will appear, which no man knoweth until it is seen (D&C 88:93; Matthew 24:26; Isaiah 40:5; Zechariah 14:5–9),[22] and the Lord will come and reign upon earth for a thousand years. The government will be that of a "perfect theocracy, with Jesus Christ as Lord and King."[23]

At the beginning of the Millennium, Satan will be bound and cast into the "bottomless pit"; his influence (and that of his evil emissaries) will not be felt upon the earth while the Messiah reigns (Revelation 20:1–3).

When Christ comes in clouds of great glory (Daniel 7:13),

those who have been resurrected and reunited with their God will come with him, as will the New Jerusalem, or the righteous city of Enoch (Moses 7:63–65; Ether 13:3–4; Revelation 21:2). The righteous dead who have not been resurrected will have their graves opened and will also be caught up to meet him, along with those righteous men and women who are yet alive upon the earth. But the wicked shall remain in the grave, unresurrected until the Millennium is over.[24]

The millennial ministry of Christ will continue for a thousand years, and men in the flesh during that time will mingle with immortal beings.[25] Those who are righteous will grow to maturity and in some manner be changed to immortality "in the twinkling of an eye" (D&C 63:50–51), while those who do not merit such an instant transition will pass into the grave and await a future resurrection. The earth will be restored to the condition it enjoyed in the Garden of Eden,[26] and the enmity between man and beast will cease (D&C 101:26).

When the thousand years of the Millennium are over, Satan will be loosed from his imprisonment. He and his dark angels will again be active during the ensuing "little season," the length of which has not been revealed.[27] This "little season" will be the final testing ground of man's integrity to God. A great gathering of the forces of evil and the forces of good will take place during this time, and the final combat between the Savior of the world and the leader of darkness will take place; but the outcome of this conflict has been prophesied, and "the vanquishment of Satan and his hosts shall be complete."[28]

Ultimately, every man and woman who has ever lived upon the earth will be resurrected. The righteous will dwell with Christ and his Father in the kingdom of God forever (D&C 76:51–65), while those who are unworthy of that kingdom will find their place, as prepared by the Father. The earth will be consumed as if by fire and will pass away before it is finally restored to its celestial glory (Revelation 20:11–15; D&C 29:23; 43:32). The plan of salvation will be fulfilled with the final judgment of mankind, and Jesus Christ, our Savior and King, will finally receive his reward — he will present his kingdom to the Father, and "then shall he be crowned with the crown of his glory, to sit on the throne of his power to reign forever and ever" (D&C 76:108).

Jesus the Messiah

Placing Christ in Our Lives

Jesus Christ fulfilled his mission in all things — yet he learned obedience from the things he suffered. He was the great Jehovah, God of the Old Testament. He was with the Father from the beginning. He, along with others, met in a great council in heaven[1] and under the direction of the Father assisted in the plan of salvation. He was the firstborn of the Father in the spirit and the Only Begotten of the Father in the flesh. He was chosen from the beginning to be the Savior of the world and the Redeemer of mankind. He sacrificed his life to overcome death — which came into the world as a result of the fall of Adam — and to give the free gift of resurrection to all. He fulfilled the plan by which, through repentance and obedience, all mankind can return with him to the kingdom of his Father.

Under the direction of the Father he created the heavens and the earth while he was yet in the spirit. He and the Father created all things that live and grow upon the earth, including man. He was with the Father in the Garden of Eden when the Father visited Adam and Eve; and when Adam fell, he witnessed the Father's punishment of our first parents and understood that from thenceforth until the end of the world, all things were to be done in the Son's name. He was Jesus Christ, the Son of God, the Messiah.

Christ was born under humble circumstances, but the heavens rejoiced at his coming. Signs were given, testimonies of angels were heard, and kings came from afar to adore him. From the very beginning Lucifer feared the Savior's mission and attempted to destroy him. Through the evil one's influence Herod the Great killed the helpless infants in an attempt to also kill him.

The Gospel writers bore witness that the Old Testament prophets had foretold of his birth, and they were meticulous to note his conformity with the Mosaic Law —for he was a Jew, born under the Covenant. But of his childhood they said nothing, recording only that "the child grew, and waxed strong in spirit, filled with wisdom: and the grace of God was upon him" (Luke 2:40). The silence is broken when Luke tells the story of Jesus teaching in the temple at twelve years of age, but of his teen years and his early manhood nothing is known. They testify only that "Jesus increased in wisdom and stature, and in favour with God and man" (Luke 4:52). Their record was not intended to be a record of Jesus Christ the man but of Jesus Christ the Savior. The recorded details of his life increase at the point when the Lord came of age and began his ministry. The gospel writers commenced his ministry with his baptism and John the Baptist's witness of his divinity. His trials with the devil (which must have been related by Jesus himself) were recorded to show that he, too, had to conquer temptation. The authors of the Gospels proclaimed his Messiahship by recording miracle upon miracle, repeatedly demonstrating his consummate power and compassion; they recorded his parables — stories of everday life that encompassed the truths of the kingdom of heaven —to illustrate his teachings; and they transcribed his discourses to evidence his Messiahship and to celebrate the establishment of his new kingdom upon the earth.

Jesus took Peter, James, and John upon the mount and was transfigured before them. It was here that these Apostles received the keys of the kingdom from prophets of old; but more important, they witnessed the *glory* of the Son and heard the personal *testimony* of the Father regarding his divinity.

At the close of his mission he rode into Jerusalem as the King of kings and Lord of lords. He used *little miracles* to provide for the *little* necessities of his entrance: acquisition of the colt upon which he would ride, and the procurement of the room for the Last Supper. He celebrated the end of the old Mosaic Law and the beginning of the new gospel of salvation by eating the Passover Feast, and it was at this feast that he introduced the ordinance of the washing of feet and taught an impetuous Peter the importance of service. While at the feast the betrayer was foretold, and when Judas left to conclude his nefarious affairs the Lord introduced the sacrament, an ordinance that would replace sacrifice. The Savior's crucifixion fulfilled the need for sacrifice, for his death was the "ultimate sacrifice" for mankind; while sacrifice looked forward to his mission, sacrament looked back to his atonement, his trials, his condemnation, his crucifixion, and his resurrection.

After the Passover Feast, Jesus took the eleven remaining Apostles into the Garden of Gethsemane. He left eight of them near the entrance and took Peter, James, and John further into the Garden where they could watch while he prayed and be a witness to his suffering. But the three Apostles were fatigued, and although their spirits were willing, their flesh was weak. They slept, while the God of Heaven and Earth suffered and took upon himself the sins of all mankind—an obligation so painful that it caused him to "bleed at every pore."

Soon thereafter Christ was arrested, shamed, and tried before both the Jewish Sanhedrists and the heathen Roman conqueror. "Art thou the Christ?" they asked. "I am," he responded, and they condemned him for being what he was. He was beaten, spat upon, scourged, and mocked as the Jewish "King."

Finally, the Lord was presented to his people —the very people who for centuries had looked for the Messiah in all that they did. "Which of these two should be loosed as a boon to you on this your feast day," Pilate asked, in effect, "Jesus, your King, or Barabbas, the robber and murderer?" "Barabbas," they cried. And Jesus? "Crucify him" they shouted. The order was given! Christ was scourged, and a crown of plaited thorns was forced upon his bleeding brow. Then he was paraded through the city streets and crucified.

Between death and the Resurrection the Savior opened the doors of the spirit prison so that the gospel could be taught to those who had died without law, and he alerted his "other sheep" on the Western Hemisphere of his imminent coming. On a Sunday morning he became the first fruit of the resurrection by breaking the bands of death and overcoming the fall of Adam — thus dooming the forces of evil forever.

For forty days after Jesus rose from the grave he taught his Apostles and disciples so that they could witness the literal resurrection. Then the Messiah ascended into heaven, only to descend soon after to the disciples on the Western Hemisphere so that they, too, could witness him. But even with the personal testimony of hundreds and thousands of souls to witness his divinity, the gospel fell away and his teachings were changed. Jesus had brought a message that was not only woven into the fabric of everyday life but was eternal; yet they changed the commandments, refused to obey the "word," changed the ordinances, and rejected not only the law but also the Lawgiver.

After centuries of darkness, the Savior reinstituted his mission by opening the last dispensation of time. The gospel was restored and was again available for salvation — that all men might have the opportunity to accept him and make him a part of their lives. The time will come when he will again descend from the heavens, but this will be a descent with power wherein he will destroy the wicked and rule and reign a thousand years with the righteous.

Jesus Christ is the power of salvation — salvation is the purpose of life. Man can no more hinder the eventual course of the plan of salvation than he can rise from the dead without it. Yet it is in accepting Christ, in making him an integral part of our lives in everything we do, that we acquire the power to overcome death — both physical and spiritual. Through the Lord we can again be with the Father, for Jesus Christ is the only name under heaven whereby man can be saved — and the salvation of mankind is the mission of Jesus the Messiah.

Notes

Introduction

1. Miracles, Parables, Sermons.
2. Ed 1:145; 2:55.

Chapter 1: In the Beginning

1. MM 1:21.
2. JC p. 10.
3. A Doctrinal Declaration by the First Presidency and the Council of the Twelve Apostles of The Church of Jesus Christ of Latter-day Saints, Salt Lake City, Utah, 30 June 1916. As quoted in AF pp. 465–66.
4. JC p. 39. See also D&C 130:22; TPJS p. 345.
5. MM 1:21.
6. MM 1:23.
7. TPJS pp. 346–47.
8. TPJS p. 354.
9. JC p. 14, n1.
10. JC p. 17.
11. JC p. 17.
12. JC chapter 4.
13. JC p. 7.
14. JC p. 18.
15. JC p. 9.
16. JC pp. 6–7. See D&C 29:36–38; 76:23–27.
17. JC p. 33. See Hebrews 1:1–2; 1 Corinthians 8:6; Colossians 1:16–17; John 1:1–3. For additional references concerning Christ as the creator of this world see: Moses 2:26–27; Helaman 14:12; Mosiah 3:8; 4:2; Alma 11:39; 3 Nephi 9:15; D&C 14:9; 29:30–31; 45:1; 76:24.
18. JC p. 9.
19. A of F p. 236.
20. Ed BHOT 7:178–84; JC p. 240; see the book of Ezra.
21. A of F p. 245.
22. JC p. 42.
23. Ed 1:163.
24. JC p. 45.

25. JC p. 53, n1.
26. JC p. 54, n1.
27. Psalms 2:7; 22:1, 16, 18; 69:21; 89:8–9; 110:4; 118:22.
28. JC p. 45.
29. Sermons pp. 122–23.
30. JC. p. 4.

Chapter 2: "And the Word Was Made Flesh"

1. Farrar 1:53.
2. Smith p. 434.
3. Ed 1:225.
4. Ed 1:225.
5. Ed 1:224, n2.
6. Ed 1:146.
7. Ed 1:224.
8. Ed 1:147.
9. Geikie 1:21.
10. Ed 1:145.
11. As quoted in Ed 1:163.
12. Ed 1:160.
13. Ed 1:163.
14. Ed 1:164.
15. Ed 1:164.
16. Geikie 1:75.
17. Geikie 1:76.
18. Geikie 1:77.
19. Ed 1:178.
20. Ed 1:145.
21. Ed 1:209.
22. JC p. 84.
23. MM 1:322.
24. Ed 1:149.
25. Farrar 1:6; Ed 1:149.
26. Ed 1:148–49.
27. Ed 1:149; JC p. 89, n5.
28. JC p. 86; MM 1:316; Ed 1:149.
29. JC p. 87.

30. JC p. 87.
31. Ed 1:150.
32. Geikie 1:99.
33. Geikie 1:99.
34. Ed 1:149.
35. Geikie 1:99.
36. JC p. 84.
37. Geikie 1:100; MM 1:317–18.
38. Ed 1:151.
39. JC p. 80.
40. Ed 1:150.
41. JC p. 81.
42. JC p. 81.
43. Geikie 1:101.
44. Ed 1:191–93.
45. JC pp. 94–95.
46. Geikie 1:101.
47. Geikie 1:102.
48. JC p. 116.
49. JC p. 97.
50. JC p. 82.
51. Ed 1:152.
52. Ed 1:152.
53. JC p. 82.
54. Ed 1:152.
55. Geikie 1:103.
56. Geikie 1:104.
57. Ed 1:155.
58. Geikie 1:108.
59. Geikie 1:108.
60. Geikie 1:109.
61. Ed 1:182–83; JC pp. 91–92.
62. Ed 1:185.
63. Geikie 1:114.
64. Geikie 1:113.
65. Ed 1:180.
66. JC p. 93.
67. Ed 1:187; Geikie 1:114; MM 1:349–50.
68. JC p. 93.

69. Ed 1:186–87.
70. JC p. 94.
71. Ed 1:189.
72. Farrar 1:20.
73. Farrar 1:20.
74. Geikie 1:119.
75. Ed 1:193.
76. Ed 1:194.
77. Geikie 1:123.
78. Ed 1:194.
79. Ed 1:194.
80. Geikie 1:120.
81. Ed 1:196.
82. Geikie 1:122.
83. Ed 1:197.
84. Ed 1:199.
85. Ed 1:199.
86. Ed 1:202.
87. Ed 1:200.
88. MM 1:356.
89. Ed 1:207; MM 1:357.
90. Ed 1:203.
91. Ed 1:203.
92. Farrar 1:26.
93. Ed 1:204.
94. Ed 1:204–14.
95. Ed 1:204.
96. Farrar 1:25.
97. Ed 1:204.
98. Ed 1:205.
99. Ed 1:206.
100. JC p. 99; Ed 1:207.
101. Ed 1:207.
102. Ed 1:213–14.
103. Ed 1:214.
104. JC p. 98.
105. Farrar 1:40.
106. Ed 1:214.
107. Farrar 1:47.

108. John the Baptist was beheaded by Herod Antipas (Matthew 14:10); the Apostle James was beheaded by Herod Agrippa I (Acts 12:2).

109. Farrar 1:49.

110. Ed 1:221.

111. JC p. 111.

112. JC pp. 111–12.

113. Ed 1:227.

114. Geikie 1:161.

115. Ed 1:232.

116. Farrar 1:61.

117. Geikie 1:187.

118. Ed 1:235.

119. Farrar 1:68.

120. JC p. 114.

121. MM 1:379.

122. JC p. 115.

123. JC p. 116.

Chapter 3: The Forerunner

1. Ed 1:135.

2. Ed 1:135, n4.

3. Ed 1:135.

4. Ed 1:136.

5. Ed 1:136.

6. Ed Temple p. 157.

7. Ed 1:134.

8. Ed 1:134.

9. Ed 1:137.

10. Ed 1:138.

11. Ed Temple p. 156.

12. JC p. 78.

13. Ed 1:140.

14. JC p. 78.

15. TPJS p. 261.

16. JC p. 122.

17. Geikie 1:372.

18. TPJS p. 276.

19. Geikie 1:373.

20. Ed 1:265.

21. Geikie 2:372.

22. Ed 1:273.

23. Ed 2:272.

24. JC p. 122.

25. JC p. 122.

26. Ed 1:271.

27. TPJS pp. 335–37.

28. Ed 1:269–74.

29. JC p. 124.

30. Geikie 1:386.

31. Ed 1:277.

32. Ed 1:278.

33. JC p. 125.

34. Ed 1:278.

35. JC p. 125.

36. JC p. 126.

37. JC p. 126.

38. TPJS p. 275.

39. Bruce p. 1.

40. Bruce p. 4.

41. Ed 1:391–92.

42. Sermons p. 156.

43. JC p. 255.

44. Ed 1:666.

45. JC p. 253.

46. Ed 1:658.

47. Ed 1:660.

48. Ed 1:667.

49. JC p. 254.

50. JC p. 255; Sermons p. 166.

51. Sermons p. 168.

52. TPJS pp. 275–76.

53. Ed 1:672–74; Smith p. 581; Bible Dictionary: Herodias.

54. Ed 1:672.

55. Ed 1:674.

Chapter 4: To Fulfill All Righteousness

1. JC p. 126.
2. *Deseret Weekly News* 54:482, 13 March 1897.
3. Ed 2:745–46.
4. In these two unique baptismal circumstances no one was available to perform the ordinance for the gift of the Holy Ghost; therefore, the Holy Ghost "descended" upon them to complete the requirement of baptism both by water and by fire.
5. TPJS pp. 275–76; MM 1:404, n4.
6. JC p. 126.
7. 2 Corinthians 5:17; Galatians 6:15; Ephesians 4:22–24; Colossians 3:9–10.
8. JC p. 128.
9. Ed 1:292.
10. Sermons p. 156.
11. JC p. 133.
12. Miracles chapter 2.
13. Ed 1:302.
14. Farrar 1:122.
15. Ed 1:305.
16. Ed 1:306.
17. JC p. 135.
18. JC p. 133.
19. Sermons pp. 83–87.
20. Geikie 2:235.
21. Ed 2:91.
22. Ed 2:91–92.
23. MM 3:55.
24. Ed 2:92.
25. Geikie 2:236.
26. Bible Dictionary: Elias; TPJS p. 158.
27. JFS 2:110–11; see also D&C 110:11–16; 133:54–55.
28. MM 3:57–58.
29. JC p. 371.
30. JC pp. 371–72.
31. JC p. 373.
32. JC pp. 373–74.

Chapter 5: Sacred Times

1. Ed 1:112–13.
2. Ed 1:112.
3. Ed 1:112; 2:548.
4. Ed 1:114.
5. Ed 1:114.
6. Ed 1:120.
7. Ed Tem p. 38.
8. Ed 1:243; 2:431.
9. Ed 1:120.
10. Ed 1:116.
11. Josephus, Wars, Book vi, ix:3.
12. Miracles, p. 28.
13. Miracles, Parables, and Sermons.
14. Sermons chapter 7.
15. Geikie 2:371.
16. Ed 2:364.
17. Ed 2:364.
18. Bible Dictionary: Bethany.
19. Farrar 2:196.
20. JC p. 510; Farrar 2:195.
21. Ed 2:365.
22. Farrar 2:195.
23. The exact location of Bethphage is unknown. Some believe it to have been a part or suburb of Jerusalem, while others generalize it as a description of a district near the city. (Ed 2:364.)
24. Farrar 2:196.
25. Ed 2:365–66.
26. Ed 2:365.
27. Geikie 2:374.
28. Ed 2:371.
29. Geikie 2:372.
30. That the colt was unridden was evidence of its consecration to Jehovah, as was required of certain sacrificial animals in the Law of Moses (Numbers 19:2; Deuteronomy 21:3).
31. Ed 2:364–65; JC p. 516.
32. Geikie 2:372.
33. Geikie 2:372.
34. Ed 2:368.

35. JC p. 514.

36. Ed 2:370.

37. Geikie 2:376.

38. JC p. 514.

39. Ed 2:488.

40. Geikie 2:376.

41. Ed 2:367.

42. Ed 2:373.

43. Ed 2:372.

44. Sermons chapters 11–12.

45. Geikie 2:429.

46. JC p. 592.

47. Ed 2:490.

48. Ed 2:491.

49. Geikie 2:436.

50. Geikie 2:436.

51. Ed 2:490.

52. Geikie 2:436.

53. Geikie 2:437.

54. Ed 2:491.

55. Geikie 2:439.

56. Ed 2:492.

57. Ed 2:493.

58. Ed 2:493.

59. Ed 2:493–95; Geikie 2:438–39; Farrar 2:278–79.

60. Ed 2:493; MM 4:31–32.

61. Ed 2:494.

62. Ed 2:495.

63. Ed Tem p. 237.

64. MM 4:36.

65. Ed 2:497.

66. Ed 2:498–99.

67. Farrar 2:281.

68. Ed 2:499, n1; MM 4:37.

69. Miracles p. 99.

70. Geikie 2:440; MM 4:38.

71. JC p. 595.

72. Geikie 2:440.

73. MM 4:38.

74. MM 4:40.

75. The ordinance of the washing of feet was restored 27 December 1832 so that the Saints could be cleansed "from the blood of this wicked generation" (D&C 88:74–75). The Prophet Joseph Smith was commanded to institute the ordinance of the washing of feet at the commencement of the School of the Prophets. When the school began on 23 January 1833, Joseph Smith washed the feet of the members of the school, and "by the power of the Holy Ghost I pronounced them all clean from the blood of this generation" (HC 1:322–24; 2:287).

On 12 November 1835, after the first latter-day Apostles had been called and ordained, Joseph Smith addressed them concerning the washing of feet, instructing them that the house of the Lord then being built in Kirtland must be prepared and a solemn assembly called so that the ordinance could be attended to (HC 2:308–9). On 29 and 30 March 1836, all of the leading brethren of the Church (including the First Presidency, the Council of the Twelve, Bishoprics, and presidents of quorums) participated in the ordinance (HC 2:426–31).

76. Farrar 2:287.

77. Geikie 2:442.

78. Ed 2:509.

79. Throughout the Passover supper Jesus noted (identifying Judas and Peter individually, but including all of the Apostles in general) that certain prophecies would be fulfilled. It should be understood that the individuals involved had not been called to specifically fulfil those prophecies, but that the events which would precipitate the fulfillment were about to occur, and the filfillment would take place because of the natural choices and selections made by those parties participating in the events.

Although the scriptural statement concerning these prophecies is "that the scripture might be fulfilled," it did not mean "in order that" or "for the purpose of" the scripture being fulfilled. All things took place in the normal course of events, and each individual (including Peter and Judas) acted upon his free agency and chose to do what he did.

John records these events as happening during the Pascal meal, while the Synoptics record them as taking place after the dinner as the group traveled to Gethsemane (see chapter 7).

80. DNTC 1:718.

81. MM 4:50.

82. JC p. 594; Ed 2:504–5.

83. DNTC 1:720–21. John does not record the ordinance of the sacrament and the Synoptics do not record the washing of feet. However, they all seem to agree on the general progression of the meal. While it seems evident that Judas participated in the washing of feet, there is disagreement as to whether he participated in the sacrament. John indicates that Judas left before the sacrament was instituted. Matthew and Mark would agree with this order, although it could be inferred from Luke that Judas remained during the majority of the meal and partook of the sacrament before leaving the table. (See Luke 22:17–23.)

Some have indicated that Judas partook of the sacrament in order that he might have one last opportunity to abandon his evil purpose, or finally conclude his condemnation (JC p. 619, n2); others have indicated that Judas left the meal prior to its institution (Ed 2:508; DNTC 1:716). While this argument has persisted, no definite answer to the question can be determined from the scriptural record.

84. Ed 2:509–11.
85. MM 4:54.
86. DNTC 1:723.
87. Sermons p. 104; Geikie 2:184.
88. Geikie 2:184.
89. DNTC 1:719.
90. MM 4:52, 62.
91. DNTC 1:724.

Chapter 6: In the Valley of the Shadow of Death

1. Ed 2:533.
2. Ed 2:533.
3. Farrar 2:307.
4. Sermons p. 234.
5. JC pp. 613–14.
6. DNTC 1:774; JC p. 614.
7. Farrar 2:314.
8. Sermons p. 53.
9. Sermons p. 104.
10. MM 4:12.
11. Sermons chapter 9.
12. Miracles p. 141.
13. Sermons p. 53.
14. MM 4:18.
15. Ed 2:476.
16. Ed 2:477.
17. JC p. 615.
18. Ed 2:542.
19. Miracles chapter 11.
20. JC p. 616.
21. Ed 2:545.
22. Ed 2:573.

23. Of the four Gospels only Matthew records the end of Judas Iscariot; however, at the commencement of the book of Acts Luke notes, speaking of Judas, "this man purchased a field with the reward of iniquity; and falling headlong, he burst asunder in the midst, and all his bowels gushed out" (Acts

1:18). Assuming Matthew's rendition to be correct, factually it might have been that as the hanging body of Judas was being cut down it dislodged and fell, thus satisfying the statement of Luke's (See JST, Matthew 27:6). For another thought on the matter see Ed 2:575.

Chapter 7: The Trials

1. Geikie 2:483.

2. Farrar 2:327.

3. There are differences of opinion concerning the appearance of Christ before Annas. Some authors (Farrar 2:326; DNTC 1:782) have decided that the first public hearing of Jesus took place before Annas, with the successive two Jewish trials before Caiaphas and the Sanhedrin—then on to Pilate. Others (Ed 2:546; JC pp. 621-22) have concluded that only a private interview took place before Annas, that no record was made of it, and that the three recorded interviews before the Jews took place before Caiaphas and the Sanhedrists before the Lord was presented to Pilate. It is left up to the reader to study the scriptural text and other available writings and determine his own conclusion.

4. Ed 1:262.

5. Ed 1:112; 2:548.

6. Ed 2:541-42, 547.

7. Ed 2:546-47.

8. Ed Tem p. 34.

9. Ed 2:565.

10. Ed Tem p. 34.

11. Ed 2:566.

12. Ed 2:566.

13. Ed 2:566.

14. Geikie 2:489.

15. MM 4:155.

16. JC p. 623.

17. JC p. 623.

18. Geikie 2:487.

19. Geikie 2:499.

20. JC p. 622.

21. Geikie 2:486.

22. WMC 1:219-309.

23. Ed 1:309.

24. WMC 1:248-49.

25. Farrar 2:354.

26. Farrar 2:354-55.

27. Farrar 2:354.
28. Geikie 2:495.
29. MM 4:162.
30. JC p. 632.
31. Geikie 3:503.
32. Geikie 2:508.
33. Geikie 2:502.
34. Geikie 2:509.
35. Farrar 2:360; JC p. 640.
36. Farrar 2:377.
37. Geikie 2:514.
38. Ed 2:579.

Chapter 8: "It Is Finished"

1. Ed 2:601.
2. Ed 2:592.
3. Ed 2:582.
4. Ed 2:584.
5. Farrar 2:393.
6. Ed 2:584–85.
7. DNTC 1:807.
8. Farrar 2:398.
9. Farrar 2:398.
10. Ed 2:585.
11. Farrar 2:394.
12. DNTC 1:814.
13. Ed 2:586.
14. JC p. 667, n4.
15. Ed 2:589.
16. Ed 2:589.
17. Farrar 2:400.
18. Ed 2:591.
19. MM 4:211–12.
20. Ed 2:594.
21. Ed 2:595.
22. Farrar 2:393.
23. TPJS p. 309.

24. The women mentioned at the cross by the various gospel writers are Mary, the mother of Jesus; her sister, Salome, who was the mother of James and John; Mary Magdalene; and Mary, wife of Clopas (or Cleophas), described as the mother of James and Joses. "Thus Salome, the wife of Zebedee and St. John's mother, was the sister of the Virgin, and the beloved disciple the cousin (on the mother's side) of Jesus, and the nephew of the Virgin. . . . Nor was Mary the wife of Clopas unconnected with Jesus. What we have every reason to regard as a trustworthy account describes Clopas as the brother of Joseph, the husband of the Virgin. Thus, not only Salome as the sister of the Virgin, but Mary also as the wife of Clopas, would, in a certain sense, have been His aunt, and her sons His cousins. And so we notice among the twelve Apostles five cousins of the Lord: the two sons of Salome and Zebedee, and the three sons of Alphaeus or Clopas and Mary: James, Judas surnamed Lebbaeus and Thaddaeus, and Simon surnamed Zelotes or Cananaean." (Ed 2:602-3.)

25. Ed 2:603.

26. John's record indicates a later time, but this suggests that error has crept into it (DNTC 1:827).

27. DNTC 1:828.

28. JC p. 661.

29. Ed 2:611.

30. Ed Tem pp. 61-62.

31. DNTC 1:830.

32. Ed 2:613.

33. Ed 2:613.

34. Ed 2:61; JC p. 667 n4.

35. Ed 2:617.

36. Ed 2:618.

37. JC pp. 673-74.

38. JC p. 671.

39. JC p. 671; MM 2:242.

40. JC p. 675; AF 7:18-33; James E. Talmage, *The House of the Lord*, pp. 63-93.

41. JC pp. 675-76.

42. Sermons p. 123.

43. MM 4:245.

44. It should be remembered that there are certain individuals that are not forgiven in this world nor in the world to come. The fate of these individuals, known as the sons of perdition, is known only to God and to those who receive it (D&C 76:43-46).

Chapter 9: "He Is Risen"

1. Ed 2:621.
2. Miracles p. 104.
3. Ed 2:622.
4. Ed 2:623.
5. Farrar 2:425.
6. See Matthew 16:21; 17:23; 20:19; Mark 9:31; 10:34; Luke 9:22; 13:32; 18:33.
7. Ed 2:624.
8. Ed 2:624.
9. Ed 2:629.
10. Miracles p. 160.
11. Concerning the comment of the Lord to Mary Magdalene wherein he stated, "for I am not yet ascended to my Father," James E. Talmage said: "If the second clause was spoken in explanation of the first, we have to infer that no human hand was to be permitted to touch the Lord's resurrected and immortalized body until He had presented Himself to the Father. It appears reasonable and probable that between Mary's impulsive attempt to touch the Lord, and the action of the other women who held Him by the feet as they bowed in worshipful reverence, Christ did ascend to the Father, and that later He returned to the earth to continue His ministry in the resurrected state." (JC p. 682.)
12. Geikie 2:555.
13. Ed 2:637.
14. Miracles p. 161.
15. It appears that John had intended to end his Gospel with chapter 20 but later added chapter 21 to include the appearance of the Savior on the shores of Galilee. (Ed. 2:647.)
16. Miracles p. 162.
17. Ed 2:649.

Chapter 10: Establishing the Kingdom

1. Sermons p. 123.
2. Ed Tem p. 285; Ed 2:166.
3. Ed 2:165.
4. Sermons p. 112.
5. JC p. 721.
6. JC p. 763.
7. JC p. 763.
8. JC p. 764.

9. HC 1:75–78.

10. Mill M p. 98.

11. JC p. 780.

12. Acts 3:20–21; 1 Corinthians 4:5; 11:26; Philippians 3:20; 1 Thessalonians 1:10; 2:19; 3:13; 4:15–18; 2 Thessalonians 2:1, 8; 1 Timothy 6:14–15; Titus 2:13; James 5:7–8; 1 Peter 1:5–7; 4:13; 1 John 2:28; 3:2; Jude 1:14; 3 Nephi 26:3–4; 28:7–8; 29:2; D&C 29:9–11; 33:17–18; 34:4–8; 45:37–44; Matthew 24.

13. Mill M p. 189.

14. JC p. 786.

15. JC p. 786.

16. Mill M p. 323.

17. Joseph Smith—Matthew 1:37–43; Moses 5:13; 6:15; 2 Thessalonians 2:9–12; 1 Timothy 4:1–2; Moses 7:60– 61; 8:22–30; 2 Peter 3:5–7.

18. Mill M 395–96.

19. Mill M 396–97.

20. TPJS pp. 305, 340–41.

21. Mill M p. 578–79.

22. TPJS pp. 280, 286–87; Mill M p. 418.

23. JC p. 790.

24. JC p. 790.

25. JC p. 790.

26. Articles of Faith 1:10; AF p. 375; Mill M pp. 356, 614–15.

27. Mill M p. 695.

28. JC p. 792.

Chapter 11: Jesus the Messiah

1. HC 6:308, 473–79.

Subject Index

—A—

Adam, commanded to sacrifice, 12; fall of, 11; Jesus' atonement overcame fall of, 111

Anna, prophesied about Jesus, 32

Annas, interviewed Christ before trials, 128, 133

Apostasy, foretold, 188

Apostles, asleep in Gethsemane, 111; contention at Last Supper, 98; did not understand Resurrection, 165; fled at arrest of Jesus, 118; lack of understanding of betrayal, 100, 115; seating at Last Supper, 95

Ascension, of Christ, 174

Atonement, 107; overcame fall of Adam, 111

—B—

Baptism, authority for, 67; covenant of, 68; for remission of sins, 69; John preached, 55; of Holy Ghost, 67; of Jesus, 56, 65; principle of, 65

Barabbas, chosen over Jesus, 141

Bethlehem, Christ's birthplace, 25

Bethphage, suburb of Jerusalem, 87

Betrothal, binding as marriage, 19; described, 20

Book of Mormon, "mirrors" Christ's life and ministry, 181

—C—

Caiaphas, purpose of interview prior to trial, 133

Calvary, place of Crucifixion, 146

Childhood, typical at Christ's time, 38

Council in Heaven, 9

Creation, of earth, 9

Cross, Simon carries Christ's, 147; types of, 146

Crucifixion, 143; not Jewish mode of execution, 146; route of, 147; sign on cross of Christ, 149; type of crosses, 146

—D—

Daniel, interprets dream, 188

Death, brought about by Fall, 11

—D— (continued)

Devil, bound during Millennium, 193; cast out of heaven, 9; enters into Judas, 100; opposes plan, 9; tempts Jesus, 72; work during "little season," 194

Donkey, Christ rides entering Jerusalem, 88

Dream, Joseph receives good, 24

—E—

Earth, Jesus the creator of, 9

Elias, John the Baptist in spirit of, 79

Elisabeth, Mary visits, 23; mother of John the Baptist and wife of Zacharias, 49; testifies of Jesus to Mary, 24

Elohim, name of the Father, 8

Ezra, preserved the Law, 11

—F—

Forerunner, John the Baptist was, 45

Free agency, law of, 8

—G—

Gabriel, appears to Mary, 20

Galilee, described, 15; Nazareth in, 16

Genealogies, of Christ, 19

Gethsemane, Judas knew place, 117; meaning of name, 108

Golgotha, place of Crucifixion, 146

Gospels, diversity of, on Resurrection, 164

—H—

Heaven, Council in, 9; devil cast out of, 9; devil in, 9

Herod Antipas, Jesus before, 144

Herod the Great, kills infants, 37; visit of Magi to, 35

—I—

Isaiah, foretold Christ's birth and mission, 12

Israel, other sheep of, 179

—J—

Jehovah, is Jesus Christ, 14

Jerusalem, Christ's entrance into, 83;

Scripture Index

OLD TESTAMENT

NEW TESTAMENT

BOOK OF MORMON

DOCTRINE AND COVENANTS

PEARL OF GREAT PRICE